The Limits of Educational Assessment

Other books in this series:

The Limits of Educational Assessment

ANDREW DAVIS

The Journal of the Philosophy of Education Society of Great Britain

Printed in Great Britain by Page Bros, Norwich.
This book is printed on acid-free paper

Contents

Acknowledgements

It has taken me many years to develop the ideas presented in this book, and I have received much help on the way. Between 1985 and 1996 several meetings of the Cambridge Branch of the Philosophy of Education Society of Great Britain heard ancestors of the arguments offered here, and I am grateful for their responses. I would also like to thank those who reacted to related papers given in the 1990s in London, Glasgow, Gregynog, and in Johannesburg for the International Network of Philosophers of Education (INPE), 1996.

My particular thanks go to Richard Smith. He has been a source of creative suggestions and encouragement. He has helped me to improve at least some of my obscure passages and has prevented me from making even more grammatical and stylistic errors.

Andrew Davis
University of Durham

Preface

Nobody, looking at how education has changed world-wide in recent years, could fail to notice the growth of regimes of assessment. Pupils, teachers and headteachers increasingly face scrutiny of their achievements in standardised tests. The results of those tests, or the findings of school inspectors, can make reputations or destroy careers. Elaborate systems are devised to establish base-lines and measure value added. New information technology makes it all possible and perhaps therefore inevitable. An industry is born.

Who can argue with the need for schools, colleges and universities to demonstrate that they are doing their job? Those who are accountable for public money must open their accounts to scrutiny. Hence the newspaper supplements containing league tables of schools and local authorities, the educational equivalents of batting averages, goal difference, top scorers and recent form. Punters pondering their bets need to know these things. Teachers or parents (or even children) who are devastated to find their school has slipped from 37th to 46th place must cultivate fortitude and remember that five-year plans usually involve sacrifice and suffering. There may be a useful motivational effect here too.

Yet we all have our own experiences of examinations and tests. There were teachers who achieved good results because we did little else but practice for the test. There were examinations in which we got the answers right with little idea of what it was all about (trigonometry and calculus stir in the memory). Sometimes we may doubt, on reflection, whether what was tested was, in the longer term, really worth learning, or wonder if this was the best way to produce the lifelong learners we are now told we must all become.

Of course the new assessment industry is a sophisticated one, perhaps less flawed by the errors of the past. But the thesis which Andrew Davis advances in this book, the fourth in this series of Special Issues of the Journal of Philosophy of Education, is one which stands independent of the technicalities of any individual system. His argument is that assessment cannot *conceivably* do some of the things we expect it to do: cannot, that is, in view of certain truths about the nature of, for example, beliefs and transferability or the nature of cognitive achievements such as numeracy. In particular there cannot be the kind of fine-grained assessment that will enable us to make meaningful comparisons between schools and local authorities, if what is assessed is the rich knowledge or skills worth having and which the world beyond education hopes to find in school-leavers and graduates.

On this account, then, much (though not all) current assessment practice in education is simply muddled and counter-productive. Enormous effort and expense are being wasted. Andrew Davis's arguments are detailed and complex, and those who find them unacceptable for political or other reasons will need to rebut them with the same degree of care as he has constructed them. If he is right then radical change is needed to many aspects of educational assessment, and if he is wrong only hard philosophical thinking—and no amount of talk of accountability, or of how educationalists should confine their research to classroom practicalities—will tell us that, and why.

Richard Smith

Chapter 1
The Need for a Philosophical Treatment of Assessment

The ideological and conceptual landscape in which educational assessment is situated features varied and rough terrain. It offers no easy route to the traveller. In this monograph I intend to develop a number of sceptical arguments about assessment. If these arguments succeed, they undermine the legitimacy of much contemporary thinking about the topic. To mount the campaign effectively it will be necessary to survey the landscape, and that will be the chief task of this opening chapter. Before taking even these first steps, however, it is necessary to ask some challenging questions about the credibility of my whole project.

At the heart of this monograph is an abstract conceptual critique. Its approach may prove analytically uncompromising at times and appear relatively removed from the concerns of schools, teachers and pupils. Why, then, is it necessary to engage in such reflection? How can it possibly have implications for practical educational policy? In short, the role of the philosopher, as distinct from the practising teacher or the empirical researcher, in attending to this topic requires elaboration and justification. I want to offer a general response to this challenge immediately, and to return to the issue a little later in the chapter.

Broadly speaking the philosopher must act in this matter by assuming the role of a conceptual therapist. Such an approach was made famous by Wittgenstein. There are deep and complex conceptual mythologies underlying some everyday practices in educational assessment. Nor are we simply confronted with the difficult enough philosophical task of demythologising. Further questions arise about the motivation of those who wish to hold firmly to their perspectives and to resist the 'therapy'. How, if at all, can they be persuaded to relinquish their grip?

Thinking about educational assessment within western cultures is in some ways very extraordinary. If we are honest, many of us would admit to fundamental doubts about whether certain types of important learning can be measured, and whether in principle many of the conventional forms of assessment could possibly be wholly relevant or fair. Yet we continue to support current systems. We would back attempts to improve procedures. We are suitably shocked when irregularities in the conduct of Exam Boards are revealed, or if it appears that primary schools have been 'cheating' over their Standard Assessment Tasks (SATs). At the same time we shy away from radical reviews which might even result in relinquishing key elements of our contemporary assessment practice. We deplore them yet are loath to abandon them.

Memories of assessments linger in which we succeeded brilliantly while knowing and understanding little about the examination topic. We still burn with resentment on recalling other tests in which we were unable to do justice to our considerable competence in a subject. Or we remember 'knowing' the material in an examination and scoring highly, but we admit to forgetting it soon afterwards, never again to be able to call it to mind. We have encountered individuals who were 'good' at exams, who would not be judged by most reasonable people as having much expertise in the subjects in which they were assessed. A friend has convinced me that he obtained a good grade in General Certificate of Education (GCE) Economics by learning it up from scratch the night before. He has never claimed that he learned anything significant about economics in the process.

Problems about 'transfer' are widespread. For many people higher education is quite a challenge after their school experiences. This is not necessarily because the work is more 'difficult', though it usually is. It need not relate to the increased autonomy enjoyed by the university student. Instead, there may be an unexpected contrast between a school subject and a university subject with the same name. The students assume that they will be doing more of the 'same' in higher education, even if it is increasingly demanding. They find to their consternation that their school successes do not seem to 'transfer'. The subject at higher education level does *not* seem to be the same as it was at school. I will be arguing later that the very notion of *sameness* in this context is troubled by significant conceptual problems. The theme is discussed in great depth in Chapter 6. Another example seems to illustrate a similar difficulty. Youngsters move into employment metaphorically waving their examination certificates, only to find that employers make demands of them which bear little relationship to those associated with school assessments. Yet *ostensibly on the basis of the nature of the employment concerned* these employers will insist on employees with specific subject qualifications.

The move from school to higher education or to employment may illustrate a lack of transfer of school achievement to success in the new contexts. It is also possible to point to cases where it appears that *lack of achievement* in school does not 'transfer' to failure in later contexts. For instance, a number of individuals who do poorly in a whole range of assessment procedures during their schooling go on to become millionaires. As adults they apparently employ capacities a proportion of which were allegedly probed by their school assessments. Anita Roddick, the founder and chief executive of the Body Shop, with 1,600 shops in 47 countries, failed her 11-plus, and, having trained as a teacher, described herself as barely numerate in her first job (*Times Educational Supplement*, 1997a). Did her numeracy develop later? Did her poor school achievement fail to transfer? Or does the situation show up instead the flaws in 11-plus tests? Was she already numerate in some sense at 11 while her numeracy remained hidden from the 11-plus examiners?

Admittedly the doubts to which I have referred so far relate mainly to educational assessment in the form of tests or examinations. Examinations are of course at least as old as the ancient Chinese Empire. A focus on other kinds of assessment is comparatively modern. For instance, there is a contemporary expectation that teachers assess pupils as an integral part of the teaching process. Primary teachers might review their pupils' progress weekly, and perhaps in some ways even daily. Or again 'continual assessment' found in secondary, or further and higher, education incorporates course work and pupil participation in sessions as part of the grading system. These approaches have had less time to become familiar to us. Nevertheless unease about such trends has already begun to grow. I mention a couple of examples.

In some General Certificate of Secondary Education (GCSE) courses there has been a hint of confusion between, on the one hand, assessment leading towards a grade, and on the other hand assessment to provide important feedback on assignments from which the pupil can learn. Evidently, with time constraints on both teachers and pupils it might be difficult to maintain a rigorous distinction between course work counting towards the final grade, and course work from which pupils are supposed to learn. Arguably some assignments could be used for both purposes. Yet common sense suggests that the GCSE grade should refer in some sense to a *measurement of what the candidate knows and understands by the end of the course.* Suppose that a proportion of candidates know some of the relevant material from early on, and hence score well in initial assignments in comparison with other candidates. It does not seem obvious that the former candidates should receive better overall grades than the latter if their achievements are comparable on completing the course. What matters is the final level of knowledge and understanding. Yet if early assignments count towards the final grade, those who really need the course as a whole to escape from their initial state of ignorance are in a sense penalised compared with those knowledgeable from the beginning. Recently in the United Kingdom political pressures have thinned down GCSE course work. I am not aware that politicians were motivated by the concerns I have just mentioned.

Primary education in England and Wales has always placed a heavy emphasis on differentiation. Pupil attainment varies widely within any one class, and hence, according to the relevant rhetoric, teacher provision should differentiate between the pupils in an appropriate way. The Cockcroft Report 1982 made famous the phrase 'the seven-year gap'. The mathematical attainments of some pupils were said to be as much as seven years in advance of others in a typical top junior class. Assessment, often of an informal character and carried out by the teacher herself, has necessarily played a central role in this 'differentiation by task' approach to teaching.[1]

Recently our attention has been directed to teaching in countries such as Taiwan, where they seem to lack the obsession with differentiation. Children are taught together in big groups, with apparently little attention given to the range of attainment which presumably exists. I say 'presumably'. Yet it also seems to be being claimed that attainment ranges less widely. It is held that in these countries they lack the large 'tail' of low achievement characterising primary school classes in England and Wales, especially in mathematics. The implication almost seems to be that certain approaches to assessment help to 'create' attainment differences which they were in fact designed to detect.

Attempts to make comparisons with cultures very different from our own are controversial. Many would argue that the lessons for our own education system are far from obvious. Yet even if the necessity for caution is granted, the comparisons do seem to raise questions about the very possibility of assessment, even of the informal and ongoing type carried out directly by the teacher.

The whole topic of educational assessment can provoke passionate disagreement. Those outside the education professions are still likely to have strong feelings. Perhaps this is because most people have been subjected to assessment processes of some kind, at school if not elsewhere. Moreover politicians often seek to establish links between approaches to assessment and wider issues of educational standards and quality and this further inflames opinion on the topic. Let us sample elements of these familiar lines of thought. There is little danger of caricature. The media regularly provide even cruder versions of some of the following doctrines.

Some believe that there is a connection between 'high standards' in education and traditional written examinations. It may be argued that a necessary condition for such beliefs to be sustained is that little thought is devoted to the meaning of 'high standards'. A *definition* of 'high standards' may even make reference to traditional written examinations. A few key notions are defined at least in part in terms of each other, and a quasi-religious commitment is made to all of them.

Further, written tests, externally administered, are thought to be *fair* and *objective*. Course work elements within the GCSE examination, including some tasks differing markedly from conventional written examination questions, for a while assumed a high profile in the United Kingdom. These elements are now in retreat, having been rejected by politicians as symptoms of a dangerously subjective element in examinations. In a parallel retreat, the SATs administered to primary age children have moved away from their initial practical and activity-focused character in the direction of more formal and written tests. The change was marketed as rendering the SATs less time-consuming and more practicable for busy teachers and pupils. Nevertheless some welcome the move as a return to rigour and objectivity.

In what has now become an annual ritual, examinations, which are still for the most part 'traditional' and written, are said to be growing easier. The evidence for this claim is often simply that overall a larger and larger percentage of candidates are passing, and more and more are achieving the higher grades. The possible premisses essential for this 'argument' are rarely made explicit. The criticism of examination standards assumes that teachers cannot possibly have improved their capacity to help pupils to obtain better grades. In consequence it fails even to ask how teachers might have achieved this.

Let us ask that question now, and briefly mention two possible answers. The issues raised will be revisited later in the book. Suppose it could be established in some sense that examinations have not grown 'easier'. Then teachers might have become more skilled in developing pupils' examination techniques. Or, if there is a link between improved examination technique and 'real learning', teachers might even have improved their capacities to promote such learning.

Arguments against the possibility of rising standards may be conducted in the opposite direction, so to speak. It may be accepted by some that grade improvement could in principle reflect improvements in 'real learning'. Yet others of a more cynical outlook might refuse to believe that, for instance, the publishing of league tables, the pressures of the Office for Standards in Education (OFSTED), or even the genuine and concerted efforts of large numbers of teachers, could so rapidly effect such improvement. Equally it may appear obvious that school leavers are not overall 'better' at English, maths or anything else, and so grade improvement must represent a corruption of the system.[2]

Moreover there are still widespread covert assumptions about innate intelligence, about the 'potential' of individuals and the idea that there are only a very few with high potential. It may seem to follow from this that a significant general improvement in pupil attainment is impossible. Hence alterations in grade statistics must result from problems about examination standards. Grade 'improvement' is reclassified as grade 'inflation'.

Then again, the examination system may be thought of as a way of filtering candidates, so that only the 'right kind' of people get through to university and prestige professional jobs. With grade improvement, some of the 'wrong kind' of people start to penetrate the sacred higher reaches of society. Therefore there has to be something wrong with the grading system which allows this.

Another line of thought is linked by association to the foregoing, though it is logically distinct. Many felt that norm-referenced examinations were unfair, since candidates' grades essentially depended upon how their performance compared with others who took the same examination. Notoriously A-level mathematics turned out to be 'harder' because it was attempted by a select group of 'more able' candidates. The pupil who wished to obtain an 'A' grade had to perform better than his above-average fellow examinees. Compare and contrast this position with that of a candidate attempting A-level sociology.

Yet when A-levels moved in the direction of criterion-referencing, in the sense that candidates' grades began to depend on specific test successes, rather than how they did in comparison with their peers, this at a stroke created the possibility of grade improvement. Some then felt that the top grades were being devalued because too many people were gaining them. No longer were they restricted to a small élite. Perhaps some people value achievement as a performance which is relatively better in comparison with others. That which is sought is a *positional good* (Jonathan, 1997). What the pupil actually knows and understands falls out of the picture altogether.

Criteria for the application of the term 'difficult' tend to shift erratically and confusingly within debates of this kind. Difficulty levels might be 'measured' by the percentage of people obtaining such and such a mark, or by the intrinsic content of the test items.

Content difficulty has to be appraised by means of direct inspection of the material, perhaps by those deemed to have appropriate professional expertise and experience. Such a process is open to variation in judgements between those doing the inspecting, however conscientiously this is carried out. It is quite natural for such opinions to be tainted by thoughts about the likely percentage of pupils who will succeed on the test items in question. So norm-referencing furtively resumes its influence.

I have mentioned pessimistic interpretations of grade improvement at A-level, partly grounded in the widespread impression that real achievement has remained static, or even fallen: that the products of our secondary schools are not suddenly 'better' at their subjects. Note that politicians may be strongly motivated not to share such pessimism. For instance, the publication of league tables of test results, even at the primary level, is claimed by some politicians to 'drive up standards'. If SAT scores increase over a period of several years and any suggestions of cheating, inappropriate 'easiness' of test results, etc., can be resisted, this may well be advertised as evidence that pupils *are* learning and achieving more in some significant sense. It may well be politically convenient to assert that whatever teachers are doing to drive up test results is at the same time something which brings about a genuine improvement in learning. Such assertions depend in part for their significance on the possibility of providing an adequate account of 'genuine improvement' in learning or attainment. Moreover, when the assertions are politically motivated, it seems unlikely that those making them have any independent access to 'objective information' about improvements, or about any causal links between testing, league table regimes and such improvements.

It is daunting to look at these well-worn themes philosophically. There are so many conceptual difficulties, some of them significantly damaging to children's interests, that it is difficult to know where to begin. In this book I have had to select topics for more rigorous philosophical treatment. I have tried to choose those which have the most significant implications for teaching, learning and educational policy. I intend to argue that there is a whole series of myths and illusions about what education can achieve in relation to performance in adult society. I will contend that these myths require crucial support from certain doctrines about assessment. These doctrines will be shown to be untenable for conceptual reasons. Some of the same myths and illusions support certain approaches within school to teaching and learning, in particular to ideas about matching and differentiation. These are associated with decisions about teaching styles which might involve the choice of certain kinds of whole-class teaching, or attainment grouping strategies.

WHY PHILOSOPHY?

I believe that it is profoundly important that the conclusions for which I shall argue are supported by *philosophical* argument. Many of the claims themselves are not original or new. Some are already defended by experts in assessment and others whose research is based on empirical inquiry.

Now conclusions established on the basis of empirical evidence are essentially subject to review. They may be peculiar to particular styles of assessment, and related to current levels of technical sophistication. It goes without saying that assessment methods may be changed and developed. Sophistication levels may be improved upon. For example, devastating criticisms have been made of the validity of specific forms of written test insofar as they are supposed to assess mathematical knowledge and understanding (Cambridge Institute of Education, 1985). Investigations have cast serious doubts on the reliability of certain SATs (James and Conner, 1993). It has proved difficult to achieve really high standards of both reliability and validity in one and the same assessment process. A related issue has been the failure in practice to achieve the aim of combining two distinct assessment purposes in one process, namely that of formative and summative assessment. Some lay the blame for this attempt to square the assessment circle with the Task Group on Assessment and Testing (TGAT: D.E.S., 1988).

Defenders of the possibility of educationally acceptable and technically sophisticated assessment techniques will offer robust responses to their critics. But even if we imagine that they might be unable in the final analysis to defend successfully current assessment practices they have a fall-back position. They can acknowledge that certain assessment systems and devices may be flawed at present, but that these can and should be improved. They will accuse assessment critics of making difficulties and mischief without being prepared to come up with constructive alternatives.

My *philosophical* opposition to educational assessment of various kinds has a sharply contrasting character. It is designed to establish points of principle. My central contentions will not in any way rest upon political or value positions which might be seen as problematic. To the extent that my claims are accepted, it becomes clear that it is useless devoting money and resources to 'improve' certain aspects of assessment. There are certain tricks which assessment simply cannot bring off. It will be urged that my conclusions are not only 'unpopular' but unworldly and unrealistic. Such criticism might apply to the results of empirical research. However, it cannot be used to set aside fundamental logical argument of the kind which I intend to offer here.

If my arguments are successful, the pressure on schools to offer a curriculum dominated by 'basic' subjects should be relaxed. Space could once more be made for the arts, and for a reconstructed and more carefully thought-out child-centred approach to learning. I will say more about this later.

THE SOCIAL AND POLITICAL CONTEXT

Any substantial attempt to think about assessment in education must be located in a social and political context. Few can have failed to notice the panic about education in a number of democratic societies. The rhetoric in relation to declining standards, poor quality teaching and pupil indiscipline has become very familiar in particular to citizens of the United Kingdom. Other countries in which it may be found include the United States, Australasia, and even, in a more focused fashion, Japan (*Times Educational Supplement*, 1997b).

It is not possible to identify clearly any *single* belief and value system underlying this widespread alarm, nor to produce the evidence of decline on which the negative opinions are based. For groups with contrasting values, cultural backgrounds and political agendas are all alike infected with despondency. Even particular individuals have complex and not necessarily self-consistent justifications for critical appraisals of contemporary education. So let us briefly rehearse *some* of the possible systems of values and beliefs which may be deployed when this pessimism is defended or criticised.

Some may attach an intrinsic value to education and learning. Developing the mind can be seen as worthwhile in itself. Perhaps the subjects offered are seen as possessing inherent value. Appeal may be made to a cultural heritage, and to the argument that children have to learn to be human, that they must come to see themselves 'in the mirror of an inheritance of human understandings and activities . . . acquiring the ability to throw back upon the world [their] own version of a human being in conduct which is both a self-disclosure and a self-enactment' (Oakeshott, 1972). A deterioration in educational standards is perceived as an absence of a significant good. That perception of course requires the assumption that it is better to learn to be human in the fashion so eloquently defended by thinkers such as Oakeshott than not to do so.

What is valued may not be the development of mind and reason *per se*, but rather people's capacity to make informed and autonomous decisions as adults about the kind of life they wish to lead, about the way they conceive of others, and about the moral principles to which they wish to adhere. It may be felt that the development of mind and reason has a contribution to make to the flourishing of adult autonomy. A decline in educational standards, according to this perspective, represents a constraint on the vigour of adult autonomy.

A strand of far-Right thinking appears to link morality and educational standards. For instance (though this is of course a caricature) it may almost be held that an improvement in pupils' grasp of English grammar will enhance their performance as good law-abiding citizens, or that mastery of phonics, tables, dates in British history and so forth will in some way make communities more cohesive and caring. There is much concern about the apparent moral degeneracy of contemporary society, which manifests itself in incidents such as the James Bulger case and the Dunblane killings.

This sorry state could be addressed in many ways. It sometimes appears that the Right might even wish to include in their strategies for moral renewal a requirement that pupils work on 'traditional' skills and subjects to high standards.

Anxieties about standards could theoretically surface because of worries about the health of democracy itself. The underlying argument here would be that the citizens of a democracy should be well-informed. Indeed, they ought to be in possession of a wide range of knowledge, understanding and skills. This would be regarded as a necessary though not sufficient condition for their constructive, rational and intelligent participation in the political process. I see little evidence that current anxieties about education bear much relationship to perceptions about the state of democracy.

The perceived crisis in educational standards is often related to the needs of a modern industrial competitive economy. Employees are thought to require particular kinds of knowledge, understanding and skill to play a full part in such economies. This presumably accounts for the worries about the fact that, for example, the United Kingdom does poorly in international comparisons of mathematical attainment. Education is seen as valuable, as worth supporting with public funding, insofar as it supports the kind of attainment which is relevant to healthy economic performance. It is assumed that there is a causal relationship between the viability of the UK economy and, for instance, the mathematical attainment of its school pupils in comparison with that of other countries.

Because this view of education is widespread, I intend to make use of it in much of the following discussion. Of course, many would wish to question whether, and to what extent, education should be seen as aiming to support the needs of a healthy industrial economy. I do not wish to enter this particular debate. My strategy is rather as follows: let us assume for the sake of argument that if education can help industry to function efficiently and competitively, then this is a legitimate aim for education. ('Legitimate' might mean something like this: that serving an industrial economy does not undermine the very nature of education and that following this objective is morally acceptable.) Given such an assumption, I proceed to argue that school curricula often cannot develop in pupils specific cognitive skills, precisely identifiable, which will directly serve the needs of industry. The claim will be that that the difficulty is one of principle. This is a much stronger contention than that, for instance, schools at present are ineffective and in theory might do better.

I try to show that one of the reasons why people hold that schools should develop particular knowledge, understanding and skills directly applicable to the world of work is that they are misled by a mythology associated with assessment itself. The mythology relates to

mistaken ways in which knowledge, understanding, belief, competence, ability and other achievements are being conceptualised. Once
this mythology is seen for what it is, we can return with renewed hope
and vigour to a consideration of appropriate and realistic aims for
schools. My view is that in a deeper and richer fashion schools can
help to develop adults with the kinds of personal traits which may
among other things make them effective and productive employees.
This thought is developed at the end of the book.

WHY ASSESS?

Let us turn now to a brief exploration of some of the usual reasons
given for assessment in education, and indicate in more detail some of
the lines of argument associated with such reasons which will be
followed up in later chapters.

(1) To facilitate matching and differentiation

For many primary teachers, the most important reason for assessing
what pupils know and understand is to facilitate 'matching'. The
explanations, tasks and experiences which teachers provide are
supposed in some sense to 'fit' the current understanding of the pupils
concerned. Teachers may feel that they cannot present content and
activities of an appropriate kind and at an appropriate level unless
they know something of their children's cognitive achievements.
Arrangements for organising group teaching may also depend on the
results of assessment. Teachers may, for instance, direct 'new' work at
a particular group while the rest of the class is expected to tackle
activities relatively independently from the teacher. What counts as
'new' for pupils, and what pupils are likely to be able to achieve
without teacher attention, involve judgements requiring knowledge of
current pupil attainment.

Traditionally in the organisation of secondary schooling, and to
some degree now in primary schools, assessment may be exploited to
establish larger sets of pupils with similar attainments in particular
subjects. There is debate within the secondary sector about whether
success in certain GCSE courses is useful and relevant to pupils who
wish to proceed to A-level in the same subjects. Or it may be argued
that a particular A-level subject needs to change its syllabus, given
that there have been significant changes to GCSE courses in that
subject.

An assumption behind utilising assessment in this fashion is that
children may well be at different stages in their learning, especially in
basic subjects like English and maths. It is felt that teachers must as
far as possible maximise pupil progress in all curriculum areas by

ensuring that they continue their educational journey from their *present educational location*. A substantial part of the teacher's role in this perspective is *differentiation by task*. The teacher is in control and must make decisions about which activities will appropriately match the child's current attainments. It suggests a small part, if any, to be played by the pupil herself in setting her own level of work.

The validity of this point will depend on a clear understanding of the various ways in which teaching may be said to be matched to the cognitive levels of pupils. A critical discussion of possible senses of matching is offered in Chapter 7. It also requires that matching in these senses is possible in principle. Conventionally, assessment to improve matching is referred to as *formative*. The notion of *diagnostic assessment* adds little in this connection; it simply seems to connote a negative aspect of the process, in which children's conceptual problems may be uncovered by means of teacher observation and investigation.

Incidentally, in theory at least formative assessment might be used for very different purposes from those for which it is designed at present. It could be employed to discover the extent of a pupil's initiative, imagination or motivation rather than to pinpoint her current cognitive attainments. Teachers might avail themselves of the results of such assessment to decide on the extent to which a pupil could work on a task provided within a 'differentiation by outcome' style of teaching. Arguably expectations of the duration and quality of a pupil's concentration and of the extent to which she might work with others should depend on what the teacher knows about pupil motivation and attitude. Attempts to detect specific knowledge, understanding and cognitive skill levels need not figure in such formative assessment of attitude and motivation.

I will later argue that these wider and less traditional purposes for formative assessment ought to command much more support and attention than they do at present. Unlike many of the attempts to use formative assessment to discover in precise and rigorous ways details of pupils' current cognitive achievements, they do not suffer from major conceptual flaws.

(2) To provide feedback to pupils on their progress

Formative assessment is also associated with the idea that teachers are thereby enabled to provide feedback to pupils so that they can learn more effectively. The legitimacy of this purpose depends crucially on the nature of the intended feedback. Pupils could be told that they had concentrated well, had made a considerable effort, or had displayed an impressive imagination. They also might be informed in apparently accurate detail of the ways in which their knowledge and skills had advanced in a particular field. Where appropriate they might be advised of problems they were still experiencing. Later argument below implies that this second type of feedback must quite often depend on an unwarranted confidence about the extent to which teachers can in principle uncover precise details about current knowledge and understanding.

(3) To enable teachers to discover how effective their teaching has been

> If professing teachers are so imprudent as to claim that what they are themselves striving to put across is too elusive and too ethereal to be captured by tests or measures of any kind whatever, then they should be told — kindly but very, very firmly — to find something else to teach, something teachable. (Flew, 1987, p. 35)

Antony Flew has argued in various places that a sincere intention to teach is simply not possible unless the teacher is prepared to assess the results of the attempts to teach. I suggest that Flew's position assumes among other things that:

(a) it is actually possible to detect the results of successful teaching in some way;
(b) it is not immoral to use the methods which would be required to discover whether the teacher has succeeded;
(c) the economic cost of discovering it would not be prohibitively great;
(d) a substantial causal connection could obtain between pupils' experiences which teachers engineer, and changes deemed to be improvements in pupils' cognitive attainments, and teachers or others could be in a position to detect this causal connection;
(e) the envisaged assessment methods do not necessarily distort the nature of the learning objectives and of the relevant teaching in an unacceptable way;
(f) successful teaching necessarily will have reasonably short-term consequences or 'learning outcomes'.

To reject (a) outright would be to go further even than I am willing to do in this book. The philosopher might have something to say about (b), though I shall not do so here; (c) would be a matter for the economist and the politician; (d) involves some very complex issues. I shall not seek to deny (d), but subsequent discussion about defensible versions of constructivism has several fundamental implications. These include the following: any causal links between teacher activity and cognitive gain by pupils must be indirect; the nature of such links will vary from one individual pupil to another; the cognitive gain will be impossible in principle to identify with any precision. More will be said later about these issues.

(e) may partly involve an empirical issue. However, I have argued (Davis, 1995) that some assessment systems will necessarily distort certain teaching objectives in relation to the development of knowledge and understanding. This argument will be explored further in Chapter 8.

As I say, it would be very difficult to argue in a wholesale fashion against Flew's contention. Teaching must 'make a difference'; it must make a difference of the right kind, and we must have some hope of recognising it. I am particularly concerned to mention Flew's view early in the proceedings to help me make the point that I am not offering a comprehensive rejection of *all* styles and forms of assessment in this book.

Some seek to use Flew's views to provide broad support for assessment policies currently being pursued in the UK and elsewhere (Winch and Gingell, 1996). Assessment can never be perfect, it is said, but it is better to manage with what we have, than to attempt to make do with nothing. The latter would be the mark of the insincere teacher. My response to this move, to be explored in considerable detail in later chapters, is that much assessment as currently conceived reflects such a degree of conceptual confusion that it damages education. Even education that is merely seen as the servant of the industrial economy is distorted and stunted by confusion of this kind. It is rendered powerless to turn out employees with the kinds of qualities and achievements which might prove valuable in the work context.

Subsequent argument will have implications in particular for (f) above. As I have already indicated, I will be arguing against the possibility of identifying in any precise way the current cognitive attainment of pupils. If this argument succeeds, then the 'sincere' teacher cannot hope to express his or her sincerity by frequent assessment of the pupils to detect supposed immediate cognitive gains resulting from teaching.

(4) To measure the achievements of teachers and schools

The results of assessment may be used within schools for management to determine the success or otherwise of individual teachers. Much argument in this book implies caution in the use of such an approach. Assessment results may be employed externally to enable judgements to be made about the success of schools, or collated to assist parents in making 'informed' selection of schools. It has been appreciated for some time that raw assessment results are influenced significantly by the distribution of social class, or the proportion of pupils suffering from socio-economic deprivation within a school's intake. Hence raw assessment results may enable parents to select schools with the social class distribution they favour rather than on the grounds of the 'true quality' of the school.

Attempts are now being made to use assessment data in a more sophisticated way to determine the extent to which teachers and schools have 'added value' to the pupils in their charge. Pupils are assessed on entry to school. They are further assessed at the end of their time in the same institution. The difference between their attainments is characterised as the value which has been added to them. There is said to be considerable variation between schools with 'comparable' intakes and contexts in respect of the value they succeed in adding to their pupils.

For such value-added based judgements to be taken seriously, it has to be shown that the variation could not reasonably be expected by mere chance. Even if a school's resources, staffing and levels of personal energy could, so to speak, be held constant over a period of several years, it seems likely that the average measure of added value would vary quite appreciably from year to year. Even if the assessment devices succeed in detecting 'objective' attainment levels, cohorts of pupils simply do vary from year to year. As teachers know to their cost, there can be a 'bad run' of several years. It would also need to be demonstrated that the results of pupil assessments on entry to schools could be compared across schools. There are other difficulties: it would be in schools' interests to depress the entry scores in subtle ways (Davis, 1996b). There are also theoretical problems about comparing, which will be explored in Chapter 8.

In reality, of course, schools could never be held constant in this fashion. The school which adds value to a set of pupils from, say, 1993 onwards will in many senses not be the same school in 1997, even if still on the same site, with the same head teacher and many of the same staff as in 1993. Even if the staff were unchanged, with the best efforts in the world their qualities and energy levels are likely to fluctuate. It also must be explained just how the notion of comparability between schools covers all the variables which might significantly affect the development of pupil attainment. A further practical difficulty for some schools is the fact of considerable pupil movement between schools. Hence it might be claimed that a given school was gaining or suffering from the efforts of some of their pupils' previous schools.

Robust defenders of value-added measures will assert that schools, and indeed those to whom they might become accountable for added value results, are or would be urged to look at results over several years. They are encouraged not to attach much significance to data about a single cohort of pupils. Significant school or teacher factors in adding value may be identified, it is said, if sample sizes are increased. The probability that variations in value-added measures between teachers, departments or schools dealing with 'similar' pupils and contexts are occuring by chance is supposed to be decreased given such an approach. Yet I would want to argue that this increase in sample size is likely to exacerbate the difficulty in identifying the 'same school', or the 'same teacher', as though they have stable identities over time and across contexts. Admittedly it would be foolish to pretend that schools, departments and even individual teachers lack *any* kind of persisting characteristics. However, adequate value-added measures need to make substantial assumptions about stability which might prove difficult to justify.

A supposedly unproblematic feature of the value-added narrative is the notion that pupils are tested on entry in respect of certain knowledge and skills, and that they are assessed later in their school careers on the *same* knowledge and skills, once the school has had time to add value to them. 'Adding value' seems to imply that on entry pupils can be discovered to be in possession of a given level of something, and later can be detected as being in possession of *more* of that something. Perhaps it is thought that they know more science, that they can do 'more difficult' versions of the 'same' mathematics on which they were initially assessed, or that they are better at speaking and listening, and so on.

Many of these seemingly sensible ways of speaking in fact conceal a number of logical problems which are explored further in Chapters 6 and 7 in particular. Some of these difficulties cluster around the thought that specific knowledge or cognitive competence can be identified as persisting over time, and that its improvement may be detected with an acceptable degree of accuracy.

Measuring the success of teachers and schools ties assessment closely to the currently fashionable political theme of accountability. I explore ideas about accountability in some detail in the next chapter.

For summative assessment to be used to inform judgements about one school or teacher in comparison with another, a common language is required in which to frame the judgements. I argue in Chapter 8 that there are conceptual difficulties in the way of providing such a common language if the judgements are to be about substantial and rich knowledge and understanding, rather than about thinly characterisable performances in a carefully specified restricted type of context.

It is worth mentioning in passing that the terms 'formative' and 'summative' in relation to assessment are sometimes used rather confusingly, as though two different kinds of processes may be taking place. I comment on this briefly here to clarify my use of the terms in later discussion. On the whole formative and summative assessment are not two different kinds of assessment. The terms 'formative' and 'summative' divide assessment *purposes* up into two categories. Summative assessment purposes in particular may be further subdivided. The title of this section, relating to the measurement of the success of schools or teachers, is just one of them. Other purposes include attempts to discover whether candidates have specific skills, knowledge and understanding for a particular job and whether students have general skills and intelligence which might fit them for high status professions. Terminal examination results are employed to allocate pupils to further or higher education.

Now it is true that if a strong emphasis is placed on the provision of feedback for pupils in formative assessment, then a particular process is implied, namely appropriate kinds of interactions between teachers and pupils, which will not be found in summative assessment. It is also true that summative assessment, particularly in respect of older pupils, is as a matter of fact associated with formal written tests which are often externally moderated. But there is no necessary link between written formal tests and summative assessment. Formal written tests could be used as part of formative assessment, though I have already indicated that I will later explore the fundamental philosophical obstacles to the viability of such procedures. On the other hand, a series of more informal observations of pupil behaviour, responses to tasks and contributions to discussions which might constitute a formative assessment record could also contribute to summative assessment. The formative assessment records could be summarised and levels awarded. Indeed just such a procedure is required by the National Curriculum assessment regulations in England and Wales. Again, the problem about an appropriate common language arises, if teacher assessment is to hold its own with assessment delivered by the SATs which are externally marked and moderated and increasingly dominated by paper and pencil tasks.

That concludes the initial survey of assessment purposes. I have begun to indicate some of the lines of argument to be followed later in the book. It will be useful at this point to indicate in summary form the structure and content of the subsequent chapters.

SUMMARY OF THE ARGUMENT TO FOLLOW

Chapter 2 discusses appropriate educational objectives in a modern industrial society, and the ways in which the state in many developed countries now seeks to hold education to account for the levels of skills 'relevant' to industry. To aid the exploration of these issues, some space is devoted to a direct consideration of conceptions of accountability and of the possible consequences of adopting particular forms of it.

Standards of literacy and numeracy are widely held to be too low and it is felt that schools should strive to do something about this. A careful examination is made of these two key instances of 'basic' competencies. It is shown that an industrial economy requires that they incorporate 'rich' knowledge and understanding which may be used and applied in a flexible range of contexts. The complexities of 'using and applying' are themselves analysed. This discussion then results in a fairly detailed account of what literacy and numeracy would be, if they really could be acquired and retained by pupils. In later argument, particularly in Chapter 6, I claim that some of the central components of a literacy and a numeracy rich enough to be relevant to the modern economy are to a degree mythological. When we construct a conception of a cognitive achievement such as numeracy, and think of it as something which can be acquired at school and used in the workplace, we are to some extent inventing something which cannot really exist.

Chapter 3 deals with epistemological foundations. By the end of Chapter 2 it becomes clear that to characterise fully my central ideas of 'rich knowledge and understanding' it is necessary to provide a philosophical account of the idea of 'connectedness' in knowledge. To tackle this metaphorical theme, appeal is made to 'holist' traditions in recent analytical philosophy. Possible holisms are surveyed, including holism about properties, propositions and content, meaning, and belief and concepts. Richard Skemp's well-known and helpful distinction between instrumental and relational understanding is located within these perspectives.

In Chapter 4 the philosophical scene-setting continues, with the development of an account of belief which does not favour the traditional emphasis on pupil language in educational assessment. According to the loose dispositional/functional account of belief outlined in this chapter, there is no objective fact of the matter about whether anyone holds a specific belief.

Chapter 5 moves away from the fairly technical discussions of Chapters 3 and 4, to draw out implications for the principled limitations of educational assessment in the light of earlier accounts of knowledge, understanding, holism and belief. It tackles problems about written assessment in particular, before continuing with a more general critique of the suggestion that the character of a pupil's rich or proper knowledge or skill can be precisely determined through assessment. It is not that we are bad at assessment, although we may be. It is rather that that rich or proper knowledge lacks the definitive and specific character which would be required if its presence were to be detectable by standard educational assessment devices. At the end of this chapter it is noted that teachers can only introduce and assess knowledge and skill in a limited range of contexts, and the classic problem arises as to whether pupils can manifest that knowledge in new contexts.

Chapter 6 treats this classic problem of transfer in some depth. The related issue of trait discourse, which refers to alleged psychological items such as abilities, competencies and skills, is discussed. It is concluded that much of this discourse in educational contexts, where rich or proper knowledge and skills are prominent, is mythological. The conception of a trait appears to appeal to a model in the physical sciences employed to cover the powers and dispositions of substances. It is shown how this model is inadequate when transferred to the description of human performance and cognition. Much attention is devoted to the theme of rules and rule-following, with inevitable reference to Wittgenstein. Writers in the Situated Cognition tradition have been developing claims in different terms which directly bear on the topic of transfer. This point is brought out in some detail.

In Chapter 7 the fruits of the assessment critique are applied to a pedagogically crucial principle, namely that teachers should attempt to match their teaching to the attainments of their pupils. It is shown that precise matching is impossible in principle for much of the subject content with which education is concerned, even given a varied and reasonably sophisticated account of the range of possible senses of the term 'matching'. Some discussion is devoted to the notion of sequence in learning, and to the idea of 'difficulty'.

In the light of the negative conclusions about the possibility of matching, a fresh look is taken at questions about the organisation of teaching and learning. Issues of attainment grouping, and of the desirability of certain forms of whole-class teaching, are examined. Some support is offered for a new emphasis on whole-class teaching. It is also suggested that pupils and students should be given more control over their own learning, a child-centred theme from the 1960s which *prima facie* may not seem to fit well with whole-class teaching methods.

Assessment is sometimes held to support a public language in which the achievements of pupils and schools can be reported. Chapter 8 argues that the role of criterion-referenced assessment in supporting this language is dubious, unless we restrict ourselves to describing 'thin' knowledge and skills. To secure agreement between teachers and schools about the meaning of standard characterisations of pupil achievement, reference has to be made to detailed task descriptions or test performances. This has the effect of distorting the meaning of the standard characterisations where they purport to capture rich or proper knowledge and skill. To develop this argument, ideas about reliability and validity are scrutinised at some length. The fruits of the discussion are also applied to the competency-based assessment systems being imposed on teacher training, at least in the United Kingdom.

In the final chapter, I ask whether there is a future for assessment and accountability. This depends on which educational aims are supported, and at this point in the book I allow myself to look at ultimate aims which go beyond the serving of instrumental ends in a modern industrial economy. The demands of democracy, and of a modest constructivist account of learning, do favour the continuation of some forms of assessment, and these are explained.

NOTES AND REFERENCES

1. The distinction between 'differentiation by task' and 'differentiation by outcome' approaches to lesson planning will be familiar to readers in the United Kingdom. It is not a philosophically watertight distinction, and in Chapter 7 it will be necessary to revisit it. For the present, a couple of examples should suffice to illustrate the idea. If a teacher with a range of maths attainment in her class seeks to offer maths problems at varying difficulty levels, the hardest to those with the most advanced attainment, the easiest to those with the lowest achievement, and so on, in an attempt to match current pupil understanding with work set, she is said to be differentiating by task. On the other hand, if a teacher asks a large group of children to write a story, knowing that their writing capacities differ, and expecting that some stories will be of much higher quality than others, she might be described as differentiating by outcome.

2. I heard the experienced and successful headteacher of a very large primary school tell a government education minister that his school's SATs results for both Key Stage 1 and Key Stage 2 had gone up impressively each year. He proceeded to inform her that he and his staff were also certain that the children's learning had in no way improved. The minister responded that the SATs would be retained because the public 'understood them'.

Chapter 2
Accountability and the Economy

For the sake of argument a utilitarian conception of education as serving a modern industrial competitive economy is being assumed in much of this book. In what ways may education be held to account within this perspective? What kind of knowledge is likely to interest those with the fortunes of the industrial economy at heart? In particular, which versions of literacy and numeracy would be considered 'relevant'? I now argue that both the state and employers are likely to expect literacy and numeracy to incorporate crucial elements of 'understood' knowledge. Moreover their attention will only be excited by attainments which can be 'used and applied' in real-world employment contexts. I will eventually be questioning whether such expectations are wholly intelligible, but that is a task reserved for later chapters.

I refer to knowledge which is understood, usable and applicable as 'proper' or 'rich'. This raises a number of important questions about the nature of proper knowledge and understanding, and the possible interpretations of 'using and applying'. I begin to address these issues at the end of the chapter, and continue in Chapter 3. This treatment will be essential for later analysis of the inherent limitations of various kinds of educational assessment.

ACCOUNTABILITY

Some time ago accountability was believed to take at least two distinct forms (e.g. Sockett, 1980). Teachers could be held to account for the *outcomes* or *results* of their work, or alternatively they could be called to account for the *principles* according to which they engaged in their professional practice.

The distinction between teaching for learning outcomes and teaching according to 'principles of procedure' was made prominent in educational debate by writers such as Stenhouse (1975) who attributed the distinction to R. S. Peters. The Behavioural Objectives school, particularly influential in the United States in the 1950s and 1960s, required teachers to formulate objectives for their teaching in terms of changes in their pupils which could be readily detected and measured. It was felt that the kinds of transformations which unproblematically met the requirements were observable alterations in pupil behaviour. Stenhouse feared that this approach could make way for 'performance contracting', which he claimed had in effect already been trialled in Victorian Britain through the 'payments by results' system. Inspectors visited schools and assessed pupils according to pre-specified 'standards'. Stenhouse held that the demand for teachers to formulate measurable objectives 'is part of a political dialogue rather than an educational one. It is not about curriculum design, but rather an expression of irritation in the face of the problem of accountability in education . . . politicians will have to face the fact that there is no easy road to accountability via objectives' (Stenhouse, 1975, p. 77).

It became fashionable at this time to oppose the possibility of judging teaching quality by reference to narrowly defined learning outcomes. The landscape became populated by exotic 'holistic' approaches informed by the insights of anthropology; the term 'illuminative evaluation' applied to case studies of classes, schools and experimental curricula was often used during this era. However, after the political scene in the United Kingdom became dominated by the political Right at the end of the 1970s, the role of accountability with reference to learning outcomes gradually increased. More recently, at least in the UK, 'learning outcomes' have been identified with the results of National Curriculum tests and public examinations.

Just lately there are signs that those who hold education's purse strings may wish to go further still. Teachers may be required to account for whether they have 'covered' specific curriculum content *in an appropriate fashion*, e.g. made sufficient use of phonics to teach reading. They may have to explain whether they have used approved teaching techniques, e.g. the due proportion of whole-class teaching methods. In short, their 'principles of procedure' could be monitored by those who hold financial and legislative power over their activities.

This is not the place to speculate on the real motives of those who are requiring teachers to be accountable for learning outcomes. However it is easy to see why they are unlikely to be satisfied with learning outcomes *per se*. They will have opinions, whether based on evidence or otherwise, that some *principles of procedure* rather than others are most likely to maximise learning outcomes. OFSTED makes much play with the argument that results vary considerably from one teacher to another, even when type of pupil, school, socio-economic background and the like are held constant. They cast around for other factors which might make a difference, and without too much difficulty arrive at the teaching methods actually employed. Much use is currently made by government ministers, OFSTED and the Teacher Training Agency of the phrase 'the methods that work'. According to this rhetoric, teachers should be using these methods, and student teachers ought to be taught them. I mentioned above the characteristic examples of whole-class teaching, and the use of phonics. 'Principles of procedure', then, could be regarded as covering both generic features of teaching, and specific aspects of the ways in which particular content and skills are taught to children.

Accountability for learning outcomes is being extended to incorporate accountability for methods also. In this process, the defenders of 'hard-nosed' forms of accountability are able to take advantage of a strength of 'principles of procedure' accountability widely canvassed in earlier debate. This may be expressed by saying that it only makes sense to hold teachers to account for matters over which they have some direct control and responsibility. Teachers can choose which teaching methods to employ, within any constraints imposed by their context. They cannot 'directly' decide what attainments their pupils are to achieve.

Consideration of learning outcomes is not the only source of justification for selecting methods or principles of procedure. Independent moral factors will also be relevant. Moreover defenders of educational aims other than the utilitarian may be inclined to apply criteria to the appropriateness of the 'process' which could relate to the degree of pupil involvement or control, the level of pupil–pupil interaction and so on.

Such thinking points to the possibility of other conceptions of accountability. Indeed, some have been defended. For instance, accountability could be linked to the teacher's professional decision-making in how best to deliver a 'liberal' education, in which the teacher exercises essential autonomy and is accountable to herself (Bailey, 1980). This assumes that the state has given teachers the responsibility for working as best they can to ensure that pupils receive a 'liberal education'. That phrase has many uses; in this context it implies that the task of education is to promote the development in pupils of 'rational autonomy', an educational aim which may not be compatible with the utilitarian conception of education assumed in much of my discussion.

One of the main contentions of this book is that putative specific learning outcomes often do not 'exist' in the sense required by modern systems of assessment and examinations. Hence they cannot be properly assessed or measured. So the current concentration on examination or test results is misguided, even when viewed from the perspective of those chiefly interested in the health of a competitive industrial economy. In some ways my discussion rehearses yet again, albeit in modern and more complex dress, the debate twenty or thirty years ago about behavioural objectives.

If the above claims are accepted, space is made once more for a consideration of non-utilitarian reasons for selecting appropriate teaching methods, and for returning a measure of autonomy to teachers to make their own decisions in the particular teaching contexts in which they find themselves. Several chapters will be required to develop the negative arguments before we shall be in a position to consider such matters in more detail.

At present, accountability for learning outcomes looms large. Economies worldwide are fragile. There is increasing pressure to justify the large sums spent on education. 'The various scarce resources employed within the welfare state apparatus as a whole do have alternative possible uses, both within and outside that apparatus' (Flew, 1987, p. 38).

One way of holding education systems to account is through assessment. The story goes like this. Pupil attainment can be measured. Thus the performance of schools, teachers or Local Authorities may be compared. If the currently fashionable criterion-referenced approach to assessment is adopted, then the state can expect to learn from assessment results about what children actually know, understand and can do. If the state believes that it can discover this, and assumes that attainments result at least in part from state education, it may well conclude that it is in a strong position to judge whether it is obtaining value for money. It may draw conclusions about how the education system as a whole is performing, and also about the relative effectiveness of elements within that system.

One reason for the state focusing on the indications which assessments apparently give of pupils' knowledge and skills is that these are thought to carry over into employment. Expenditure on education can be justified according to this perspective if it supports the flourishing of a modern industrial economy.

Pressure on the education system to support the economy is a familiar phenomenon in the United Kingdom and in other countries in the developed world. It has seemed to become particularly intense when the economy is frail. Beck (1981) refers to several periods in the UK when employers have attempted to reform the education system to this end. The 1880s saw science and technical education being extended and the 1920s spawned worries about literacy standards and a plethora of official reports. Attitudes about the 'basics' hardened further from the mid-1970s, and this doubtless had something to do with the oil crisis. Towards the end of the millennium the UK's industrial base continues to decline, and its standard of living in relation to other developed countries is steadily deteriorating. At the same time there is unprecedented cross-party support for the improvement of standards in 'the basics', together with emphasis on the development of procedures to monitor this.

ASSESSMENT, ACCOUNTABILITY AND VALUES

It is clear that the state *de facto* possesses the power to demand that education should assess school pupils, and further and higher education students, and that assessment information be passed to the state and to the general public. The state can insist that the education system seek to develop in pupils the knowledge which it feels will be useful to the economy, and can demand that the education system should justify its expenditure to the satisfaction of the state. Possession of such power does not settle the question whether the state has the *right* to demand that education render an account for money spent in this way.

Some would contend that the provision of financial support itself justifies that account be made by the beneficiary to the paymaster, and that this claim needs no further argument. However, for a number of reasons the application of this principle to state support for education seems a little simple-minded. First, it assumes that the 'state' is entirely distinct from the beneficiaries. Yet teachers, and ultimately pupils in a democratic society, are also voters and tax-payers and thus in a sense are themselves part of the state. Second, even if the principle could somehow be established, the right to demand that education renders an account of some kind for money spent could not be said to exist in isolation from other value considerations. Such considerations might outweigh the reasons for being accountable to the holder of the purse strings. If, for instance, the state paid for an immoral enterprise, evidently the mere fact of payment would not give the state the right to insist that the enterprise should flourish according to criteria which it had laid down.

Education might be in a position to facilitate the development of moral virtues, but if subjected to a certain kind of accountability regime would be forced to give a low priority to these virtues. The question then would arise as to whether the fruits of pursuing a vigorous accountability outweighed the potential flourishing of moral virtues in pupils. The fact that the state does possess the *power* to demand an account cannot exempt it from the requirements of morality and rationality. After all, there might be compelling arguments to the effect that it is morally imperative that children should be educated and that the aims of their education should be *other than* the support of a competitive economy. I do not intend to explore such arguments in this book, but the state cannot 'decide' that it is in principle exempt from considerations of this kind.

Even if we accept for the sake of argument the legitimacy of the demands of an industrial economy, we cannot set aside basic moral imperatives concerning the quality of teacher–pupil interactions. Let us concede that the nature and strength of these imperatives cannot easily be resolved, and that there may prove to be intractable disagreements about the ways in which pupils as human beings should be treated, arising from rival views about the nature of personhood. Nevertheless, it would be a rash thinker who set economic advantage as the indisputable victor, trumping basic moral imperatives about how people should be treated. The relationship between claims arising from economic health and from moral obligations towards individuals is likely to be complex and resistant to analysis. We are in the very difficult territory of incommensurable values, where there does not seem to be a set of rules or criteria according to which we can judge the strength of one claim against another. But this is not to say that no conflict might exist.

Similar issues arose in the debate about whether the UK should sign up for the Social Chapter of the European Union. The Chapter is relatively slim to date, but incorporates the right of workers not to be compelled to work more than a 48-hour week. The political Right argued that the UK should not sign up for the Chapter, since it would damage the competitiveness of the UK economy. Some on the Left conceded the possibility of damage, but contended that competitiveness was not the only aspect of the situation to be considered. They felt that the health of the economy had to be balanced against a range of moral imperatives. They accepted that to a degree an economy cannot compete with total success against a rival who fails to subscribe to certain moral principles, e.g. relating to the health, welfare and basic freedoms of its workers. In short, a moral and caring society might be unwilling to run the most ruthlessly competitive economy.

I happen to think that education *should* be a great deal more than the servant of competitive economies, but I do not wish my argument to depend on such a value presumption. This exercise in self-restraint should enable me to conduct the discussion on the home ground of my opponents. That way I hope to be able to put forward reasoning which they will be forced to accept, rather than providing them with the opportunity to accuse me of assuming value positions whose strength I cannot persuade them to recognise.

It is worth mentioning at this point a couple of arguments which assume utilitarian values, but which suggest that these values may be undermined in an education system which does not also cultivate certain moral or democratic dispositions in its pupils.

Certain kinds of vigorous accountability regimes seem likely to promote teaching methods which put a low premium on key pupil dispositions. These include regard for others, concern for truth and a fundamental respect for others as citizens of a democracy. The regimes I have in mind are familiar enough. Schools can be subjected to enormous pressures to achieve test and examination results. The publication of league tables of such results, and the link between 'success' on these measures and finance, will exert overwhelming influence on the kinds of priorities teachers will set in the classroom. Or again, if the state places basics such as literacy or numeracy in the centre of schools' action plans, asserts explicitly that 'standards' in these basics must improve, and that schools who do not deliver will be regarded as 'failing', teachers may be less likely to emphasise the cultivation of moral dispositions in their pupils.

Yet even a minimally democratic state may well depend for its survival on pupils developing into adults having these dispositions in some measure. Hence it could not afford to dismiss concerns about the effect of 'tough' accountability regimes out of hand. Ultimately it would be an empirical question whether a given accountability regime did indeed have a damaging effect on the health of pupil dispositions important to democratic functioning.

Questions might also be raised about whether the absence of these dispositions is likely to impede the functioning of a capitalist economy. Again, on the whole these appear to be empirical issues. Some moral dispositions, for instance relating to honesty, trust and co-operation, appear to be required for the operation of the market. Discussion of the nature of the required dispositions looks to be at least in part the province of the philosopher. It is still an empirical issue how far schools and other educational systems can be held to account in a very tight way for pupil learning outcomes while leaving room for the inculcation in pupils of this minimal morality. I do not intend to pursue these particular themes any further just now. However, they do serve to raise one or two other points about accountability and assessment which may appropriately be dealt with here.

ACCOUNTABILITY, INFLUENCING TEACHER BEHAVIOUR AND PUPIL ATTAINMENT

Suppose a system which emphasised the role of assessment in making teachers accountable was able to show that an individual teacher was making a significant difference to pupil performance. How would we identify which aspects of the teacher's performance were causally effective? This would presumably be a matter for empirical research. Bitter experience of investigations of this kind suggests that the complexities of the contexts concerned, and the variety of variables which are likely to affect pupil learning, undermine the possibility of there ever being secure results. Medley (1984) summed up some of the difficulties here. If we try to measure how much a class learns from a teacher, there is a host of variables to be considered which operate independently from the teacher yet also affect learning outcomes. We do not in fact know enough about these variables to measure them all, and it would be too expensive to do so if we did.

Even if we set this challenge to one side, if we claim to have measured how much a particular class learns from a teacher, we imply that a similar measure with a different, 'similar' class would give a consistent result. However, apparent variation in learning from class to class arises at least in part from errors of measurement. Medley points out that these 'errors' are substantial, arising from the fact that the most sophisticated assessment devices available will still possess a degree of unreliability. The 'same' assessment will not infallibly provide the same results across more than one group of 'similar' pupils.

Be that as it may, if we could identify the salient aspect of teacher performance, is it entirely obvious that it is morally acceptable to use this knowledge to effect changes in pupil performance? Surely we would need to consider a number of aspects of the situation before finally taking action. For instance, some would argue that at least to a degree the pupil has a right to exercise some choice within the educational process. The teacher's causing of changes in pupil performance would need to be compatible with any fundamental pupil rights to act as free agents. This type of argument would rest on *moral* considerations, rather than appealing to a particular conception of education. Others of course do not find arguments for these kinds of pupil rights in any way compelling. At the same time even they must accept that the degree of detectable cognitive improvement cannot be the only criterion to which appeal is made when passing judgement on teacher performance.

If we could identify what aspect of teacher performance made a difference to the results of assessment, would it be legitimate to require all teachers to produce performances of this type? If so, teachers become technicians, putting into effect the objectives and methods laid down by others. So long as teachers were doing what they were told, there would then be a sense in which they could no longer be held to account for pupil performance. The burden of responsibility would shift to those who designed the 'teacher-proof' or even 'pupil-proof' learning packages.

In the UK there is evidence of moves towards an approach of this kind, especially at primary school level. The National Numeracy Project and National Literacy Projects seem likely to produce very prescriptive materials for teachers to implement, and for which they could scarcely be held responsible. Extreme illustrations of this approach are the teaching scenarios prepared by *T3 Mathematics*

(Jennings and Dunne, 1997). Pupils face the front in whole-class teaching mode, and the teacher follows a set script with fixed resources. Pupils are often required to respond as a whole group, reproducing teacher language in a precise fashion. (At present these scenarios have no official status in the UK.)

Having claimed that those implementing teacher-proof materials can no longer be held to account for pupil performance, I should add that in somewhat nightmarish circumstances this might not be entirely so. If value-added measures of the kind referred to in the first chapter were comprehensively resourced and implemented on a national scale, it might appear to be possible to compare teachers using the 'same' materials, with strictly comparable sets of children in comparable contexts. Suppose that results still varied appreciably between teachers in the same contexts. Then the teacher who performed worse than her peers might be held to be *personally* inadequate in some way. There would be nothing left to blame except the human being at the heart of the process. Again, confidence in the right to blame would require informed certainty about the limits of chance variation in pupil 'performance', even given the possibility of strictly comparable contexts, and even if the results were measured over several years. How sure could we be that innocent and professionally competent teachers were not being unfairly stigmatised if anything like this came to pass?

These thought-experiments place a good deal of weight on the possibility that assessment methods could deliver certain kinds of information about aspects of teacher performance. In later chapters I argue that assessment often cannot in principle show that particular methods produce specifiable improvements in pupils' possession of key areas of rich knowledge and understanding.

Such arguments will need considerable space for their full development. There remain one or two other points which can be made quickly about the possibility of identifying effective elements in teacher performance. For instance, the teacher might be advancing performance at the expense of long-term pupil motivation. It is very unlikely that a method that 'works' will motivate all pupils. In the short term, motivation problems might well not show up in the results of assessments. Can we be sure that the fact that some children never voluntarily pick up a book after the age of nine or ten is unrelated to the way they were taught to read? A competitive economy cannot afford to ignore issues of motivation.

Note another familiar area of unease in relation to assessment. The teacher, or even the designer of teacher-proof and pupil-proof packages, might have discovered effective means of 'teaching to the test' which bypass proper knowledge and understanding. The usual candidates for the learning substituted for 'proper knowledge' include procedural learning, children memorising rules and facts and learning in which children are virtually conditioned not to try to 'understand', since that might interfere with high performance on the tests.

Debate about teacher-proof materials and the problem of teaching to tests has a venerable history, and in many ways it is depressing that it is necessary once more to revisit the arguments. The Revised Code of 1862, incorporating the payment-by-results system, told teachers in considerable detail what to do, the content to cover and the time to spend on it, and what was required for children to pass. Carr and Hartnett (1996) quote Matthew Arnold's comment: 'The great fault of the . . . famous plan of payment by results is that it fosters teaching by rote . . . the teacher limits his subject as much as he can and . . . tries to cram his pupils with details enough to enable him to say, when they produce them, that they have fulfilled the Departmental requirements, and fairly earned their grant'.

We are not ready at this point in the discussion to take this issue any further. In later chapters, the concept of 'proper knowledge' will be explored in depth. The strength of the perennial arguments against 'teaching to the test' will be examined in detail. Education and assessment have in many ways travelled far since the Revised Code, but we will see eventually that the original difficulties surface once more, albeit in more sophisticated guise.

WHAT DOES THE INDUSTRIAL ECONOMY NEED? THE MYTHOLOGY OF LITERACY AND NUMERACY

As was observed above, it is assumed by current assessment practices that schools can foster knowledge, skills and understanding which transfer into employment. This book argues that such an assumption incorporates considerable elements of mythology. One of the first stages of the argument is a closer study of this allegedly transferable knowledge. What kind of knowledge, understanding and abilities then might be thought to distinguish suitably endowed job applicants and to derive from their schooling?

Consider numeracy. The majority of an adult employee's arithmetic problems will not precisely resemble his school exercises. Only if he is flexibly and intelligently numerate is he likely to be found useful. To quote terms to which we will need to devote much space shortly, he will be held to need 'rich knowledge' or 'proper knowledge' of number. He should be able to apply numbers to a wide range of subjects and practical situations, grasp arithmetical operations and their interrelationships, have a sound understanding of place value, decimals and of the way number can be used to define measurable quantities. He requires a range of estimation skills, and a sense of which arithmetical operation to apply to a given practical problem. Incidentally, these capacities also appear to be essential for the intelligent use of calculators and computers. In addition some employees need to be able to communicate information using mathematics. For instance, they may need to make use of statistics and data displays. If ex-pupils either can only perform mathematical operations in a very limited range of contexts which closely resemble those in which they were trained at school, or can achieve success only in disembedded symbolic contexts, but cannot relate this knowledge to real-world contexts (e.g. they can only perform calculations on paper), then it is difficult to imagine that they could be of use in any work context.

When we come to tell the corresponding story for literacy, we again have something of a contrast between theoretical and practical knowledge, echoing the difference between pure abstract knowledge of number and its use and application.

Literacy inevitably includes a range of writing skills. These would include, for instance, capacities to spell and to punctuate. Pupils quite often manifest some proficiency on spelling and punctuation exercises unrelated to 'real' writing contexts. Teachers are very familiar with the tendency of such proficiency not to manifest itself when pupils are finally confronted with these 'real' contexts. The problem here may be characterised as competence with a narrow range of contexts, but incompetence with a wider set. In mathematics we might also encounter this type of variation in competence, but there is more to say about a contrast between 'pure' knowledge and knowledge which can be 'applied'. This topic is pursued further in the following section.

At any rate, a literate employee might be called upon to write about infinitely various subject matters, and for a range of audiences. The standard of her prose should not be affected by its subject matter, unless this happened to be highly technical. Similarly, an employee may need to read forms or three thousand word reports with equal facility. She might be expected to read paragraphs about the technical specifications of a fork lift truck, or even Jane Austen, depending on her job or profession. 'Reading' would have to involve an efficient extraction of meaning, enabling the reader to offer the material in a different form from the original text, using either the written or spoken word. The literate employee would constantly be showing her mastery with tasks and in contexts which did not resemble closely, or even did not resemble at all, the opportunities provided at school for developing literacy.

Both numeracy and literacy as outlined here essentially involve *use and application*, and a notion of '*rich*' or '*proper*' knowledge. I now propose to consider each of these ideas in turn.

USING AND APPLYING

It is not always appreciated that the phrase 'using and applying' does not cover a clearly identifiable and homogenous set of relationships. Indeed I would argue that use and application can cover a number of *importantly different* ideas. In this section the point is first elaborated through a series of mathematical examples.

'Applying to' can mean 'directly modelled by'.

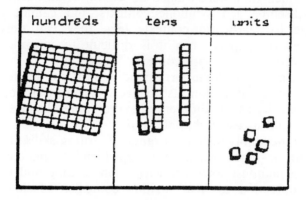

Figure 1.

Thus in the above figure of a very familiar type, so-called 'Dienes' apparatus in the form of 'hundreds' squares, 'tens' sticks, and units portrays numbers and the base-ten place value system.

For a young child, 6 may be indicated by six sweets, or six sounds. It also may be thought that simple arithmetical operations can be 'directly modelled'. Subtraction on this view could be portrayed by a situation in which some of the children in a group leave the room. Addition might be illustrated when a child who already has some marbles is given more by a friend.

That which is supposed to represent or model the mathematics may not be directly physical, but consist already of an abstraction. Thus 6 may be represented on a number line as below.

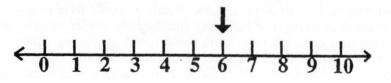

Figure 2.

The diagram appears to be a much more abstract representation of six than six real sweets. 6 is being viewed as an integer, a member of a set of numbers including zero and negative integers which cannot be represented or modelled by physical items.

Or again, 4.4 may be represented thus:

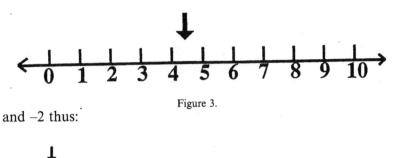

Figure 3.

and −2 thus:

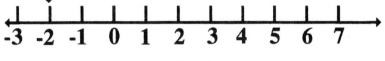

Figure 4.

Pursuing maths to a more advanced level involves grasping ideas of 'modelling' which are only very indirectly related to the physical 'mapping' instances with which we began. Examples would include the use of an Argand diagram to show a complex number.

Contrasts between ways in which mathematical items may be modelled may be studied further through the distinction between 'pure' mathematics and interpretations. For instance, Euclidian geometry may be viewed as a piece of pure mathematics, consisting of axioms and the various rules and stipulations required for the theorems to be derived. The system is satisfactory mathematically speaking whether or not it is regarded as being 'about' anything.

This geometry may on the other hand be regarded as a part of physical theory. If so, a Euclidian triangle may be represented by drawing a pencil triangle on paper. The lines as physical marks of course suffer from the limitation of having thickness, of not being precisely 'straight' (in a sense which will have to be defined), and the paper will not be a Euclidian plane. We also know that the real universe is not Euclidian, though it will pass muster for local purposes.

Compare this with the way in which six sweets model 6 for a young child. There really are six there to be counted. The representation is not a makeshift approximation for 6, whereas the triangle drawn on paper may well be thought of as a mere approximate physical attempt to portray a Euclidian triangle.

Of course it could be convincingly argued that the way in which the six sweets are supposed to represent 6 has so far been described in such a way that the true complexities are oversimplified. It is after all only the *cardinal value* of the set of sweets which is supposed to be modelled for the child. The child's attention is supposedly being drawn to the 'how many-ness' of the set, or that which the set of sweets has in common with other sets of 6 items. If the child thinks that the collection of sweets is supposed to indicate for her the concept of a *sweet*, or provide examples of cuboids, or gold-coloured items, then we have a minor pedagogical catastrophe. So even so-called 'direct' representation may require a significant level of abstraction for the child.

We need a distinction, perhaps peculiar to mathematics, between someone who can use and apply a piece of knowledge within the subject itself, viewed as an uninterpreted system, and someone who can use and apply mathematics to the real world. If this is granted, there might be richer or poorer levels of understanding of a piece of mathematics regarded as 'pure'. It is possible I think, to imagine a pure mathematician with some kind of rich mathematical understanding, who cannot use and apply their knowledge outside the subject itself.

In regard to some abstract mathematics, it is far from easy to conceptualise any notion of use and application to the real world. Consider, for instance, the proposition that any number to the power zero is equal to 1. This at first sight only seems to have a meaning within mathematics. It results from a consistent application of the notation for indices. To build up our understanding, we would probably proceed from simple cases. For example, we know and understand that $2^2 \times 2^3$ is 2^5, that $2^4 \div 2^2$ is 2^2, etc. From these basic instances, we can see why indices are added when we multiply by powers, and subtracted when we divide. This 'rule' is extended to cases like $2^4 \div 2^2 \div 2^2$ which gives us 2^0. We know that the answer is 1, which gives us a value for 2^0. But 2^0 in itself makes little sense. A number to the zeroth power? Here we have no model or metaphor to use for grasping the idea of a zeroth power. However, we can understand the rules for handling indices, and we can see that $2^0 = 1$ is a logical consequence of a consistent implementation of these rules (Davis, 1997).

Application to the world can only occur in a more indirect fashion. For instance, indices figure in more complex algebraic expressions which might be used to formulate laws of physics. However I cannot think of a scientific law which would be expressed directly with an expression involving a zeroth power.

It may be readily conceded that the element of 'numeracy' consisting of 'use and application' is unlikely to be thought to need *all* the ideas outlined above. Some of them seem obscure, and relevant only to those following higher mathematics. And yet it is not so easy to set clear limits on numeracy. Employment contexts are so diverse. They can throw up all sorts of practical problems involving number. Solving a comprehensive range of such problems seems likely to draw upon many of the notions of use and application mentioned in this section. It is not obvious that someone who can use and apply their knowledge in one way will be equally successful in an application of a different type.

Considerations about 'use and application' developed in connection with number do not hold good without qualification when we begin to think about literacy. This is presumably related to the inherently abstract character of number. Nevertheless, it may well be argued that literacy also includes elements of abstract knowledge. For instance, it may be thought that someone who is literate ought to possess a measure of knowledge about the structure of their own mother tongue. They might or might not be able to explain this knowledge directly. If they could only express it in abstract written form this would be unlikely to be deemed adequate. There would also be a requirement that it could be used in various ways when speaking, reading and writing for a range of purposes and audiences. Again, there will be a significant diversity of conceptions of use and application involved here.

Evidently numeracy and literacy can be developed in various guises and at a range of levels. Further, their precise nature is debatable and has become politicised. Be that as it may, one classic way of describing what is asked of employees in a modern industrial economy is that they 'transfer' what they learn at school to a diversity of new contexts. Much more will be said in Chapter 5 about transfer.

It may be noted at this point that the discussion in this section already enables us to appreciate the bewildering variety of ideas which could be covered by the thought that knowledge should be usable and applicable in new contexts. As I have indicated above, I will ultimately argue that the conceptions of literacy and numeracy being explained here contain at their very heart some mythological elements. Because of this, they are not assets which can be acquired definitively at school, detected accurately and comprehensively by means of educational assessment and then made use of in employment contexts. Before embarking on that argument, much work remains to be done towards the task of explaining the conceptions of knowledge that both numeracy and literacy appear to entail.

'RICH' OR 'PROPER' KNOWLEDGE AND UNDERSTANDING

A second general approach to characterising the knowledge supposedly associated with numeracy and literacy is that it is 'understood'. It is assumed that school assessment can detect whether pupils have understanding of this kind. Later this assumption will be subjected to detailed examination. I have already used the terms 'proper knowledge' and 'rich knowledge' to cover *understood* knowledge. Incidentally, there may appear to be an implication here that knowledge which is not understood is still knowledge of a kind.

Before investigating understanding, we need to refer to the traditional distinction between 'knowing how' and 'knowing that'. Conventionally examples of 'knowing how' are given as 'skills' such as knowing how to do up my shoe laces, punctuate my prose, or construct an equilateral triangle with a compass. Equally conventionally, instances of 'knowing that' are often factual, such as knowing that Faraday discovered the dynamo, that there are nine planets and so on. I do not believe that a sharp line can be drawn between the two 'kinds' of knowledge. However it is clear that people can possess items of 'knowledge that', or 'declarative knowledge', about practical matters without necessarily having the 'know-how' which it might have been hoped would accompany it. A classic example would be of someone who knows that a bicycle moves when its pedals are pressed down, but who cannot in fact do this.

This situation may be contrasted with that of someone who 'knows' something but can only 'use and apply' the knowledge in a limited range of contexts. This is not necessarily a deficiency of 'know-how'. Someone may have an item of declarative knowledge but be ill-equipped to use and apply it.

It also seems possible for a person to 'know how' to do something while owning little or no declarative knowledge in connection with the alleged skill or competence. A baby knows how to suck, and so on. Much of the know-how in which education and indeed modern industry is interested is not 'pure' know-how. It actually consists of rich marriages of knowing how and knowing that. Certainly the achievements required of the numerate or literate person seem mostly of this character. For the sake of expository convenience in what follows I will sometimes separate out knowing how from knowing that. This is admittedly an artificial procedure, and we will need to alert ourselves to any possibility that this approach might damage the strength of the argument.

It may be argued that without some understanding knowledge cannot exist at all. The situation may be illuminated through a range of examples. A child might be told by an aunt whose authority she has learned to trust that the universe is expanding. If the child is very young, her position with respect to her aunt's sentence might resemble Chomsky's infamous 'Colourless green ideas sleep furiously'. If her aunt uttered the latter sentence, the child might believe that her aunt had conveyed a truth to her. On being asked by a third party, 'What did your aunt teach you yesterday?' she might answer, 'She told me that colourless green ideas sleep furiously'.

Describing the child's state as knowledge seems a rather generous characterisation. It may be conceded that such cases do occur. In this connection I do not wish to become embroiled in sterile disputes about ordinary usage of 'knows' and related terms. However, it may be helpful to distinguish between ways in which someone's knowledge or belief may be reported. More often than not we refer to someone's knowledge in terms which they themselves would understand and accept, and omit any aspects of the subject of their knowledge of which we may think we are aware, and they are not. Consider a classic example from Quine (1960), substituting 'knows' for 'believes':

(1) Tom knows that Cicero denounced Catiline.

We know that Cicero is one and the same person as Tully, and also know that Tom does not know this. Hence we report in the above terms. Nevertheless we could make a report about Tom's knowledge in a different way, though possibly misleadingly, by saying:

(2) Tom knows that Tully denounced Catiline.

Our audience might well be misled, since they would assume that we would not say (2) unless we thought that Tom himself knew that Cicero is identical to Tully. At the same time there is a sense in which (2) is true. That which makes it true is a complex state of affairs which includes reference to more than the 'contents' of Tom's mind. Arguably we have further examples of this type of reporting in:
(3) The dog knows that its master is at the door
and
(4) The baby knows her mother is talking to her.

In (4) if we are implying that the baby has anything remotely approaching our concept of 'mother', or the idea of 'talking to', we may be stretching a point, to say the least. Depending on the age of the baby, we are probably saying that there is at least something, however rudimentary, in the baby's mind which is mother-related. The rest of our description is laid on the situation from outside the baby's mind.

The difficulty about (3) and (4) is that they are extreme cases, and for that reason some may find it less than plausible that we can report on them in this way at all. Nevertheless there are plenty of more moderate cases which are sufficiently convincing. We often report as though there is fully-fledged knowledge where the knower has only a very modest grip on the content of the particular knowledge claim under consideration.

We will need to return to the important topic of the different fashions in which someone's knowledge or beliefs may be reported by a third party. For the moment, we can say that the above examples help us to see how a child might be said to know that the universe is expanding, but more by courtesy than because the child is judged to have a significant grasp of astrophysics. The kind of 'proper knowledge', or knowledge with understanding, which will be a central focus of this book is not 'knowledge by courtesy'. For the latter is not the kind of knowledge which will be much use to employees, and it would usually be claimed that it is not the kind of knowledge the existence of which educational assessment seeks to detect.

The example of the child learning from her aunt raises another point. Given the complexity and vastness of contemporary knowledge, any one individual will have at best mastery of but a tiny fraction. It can be argued that the educated adult has an informed awareness of which people and sources should be relied upon for expertise in a whole range of areas from car maintenance to modern art. There may be one or two areas about which she knows a good deal, and concerning which she possesses a comprehensive understanding. In others her grasp will be partial, and in many instances she will only have a superficial glimmering, having to defer to experts at the first hurdle. Some may regret the fact that the renaissance polymath is not a possibility at the end of the twentieth century.

I want to concentrate on the kind of knowledge of which everyone is expected to have a thorough grasp. That is why literacy and numeracy were discussed. Evidently even these assets are matters of degree, and we would be foolish to expect everyone to possess them in the same measure. Nevertheless, there is an expectation by the state that everyone should have at least some kind of minimum competence in these areas. In the UK, evidence of such expectation includes the targets set by the government for performance in maths and English by 11 year-olds. The competence involves the direct capacities of the individual concerned, and should not require the services of experts. Jones should be able to add and subtract numbers, and apply them to contexts himself. He should not need to go to the office next to his to ask the support of the mathematically qualified colleague. I would accept that there might be cases in which someone might justifiably be described as having a degree of proper or rich knowledge, even though it was accompanied by a level of appropriate reliance upon and deference to experts. However, these are not paradigms of the kind on which I wish to concentrate here.

Before I can say more about 'proper' knowledge I need to refer to the standard conditions which must be satisfied if someone may be properly said to know something. These standard conditions have been very extensively discussed in analytical philosophy over the last few decades, but I hope that in avoiding the complexities I do not distort those matters about which there is basic agreement. Suppose that Susan knows that touching the battery terminal with the wire will make the bulb light up. It is generally accepted, then, that four conditions must be satisfied:

(1) It must be true that touching the battery terminal with the wire will make the bulb light up.
(2) Susan must believe that this is the case.
(3) Susan must be justified in believing it.
(4) A condition to defeat so-called Gettier counter-examples.[1]

The important condition for the current discussion is the third. Ayer once referred to this as the right to be sure. Often we have the right to be sure because we are relying in appropriate ways on the expertise of others, but I have made it clear that these are not the kind of cases I wish to consider here. In such instances, one might be justified in believing X while having very little understanding of it. It is perfectly possible to 'learn' facts from a teacher but be unable to do anything much with them. Pupils subjected to certain types of factual diets may be able to regurgitate facts when asked particular questions or subjected to particular narrow types of examinations or assessment. Their limited capacities to manifest their 'knowledge' of these facts would be linked to their modest understanding of them.

Where deference to experts does not feature prominently, if I am to be justified in a belief then I must have some understanding of it. Again, consideration of examples is likely to make it clear that understanding comes in degrees, that it will be virtually impossible to quantify it, and distinctive points might need to be made about the kind of understanding which might accompany knowledge in different subjects. Children's understanding in many areas will only slowly increase. There is no justification without at least a measure of understanding, but obviously the reverse does not hold good generally. I can understand something which I believe, without necessarily being justified in believing it.

LITERACY, NUMERACY AND PROPER KNOWLEDGE

To sum up the results of the discussion so far, and to illuminate some of the key points in more depth, it is worth taking our explorations of literacy and numeracy further. Within literacy we appear at first sight to be dealing with capacities, competencies and the like, rather than with bodies of declarative knowledge. To a degree first impressions are a little misleading.

Consider the ability to use full stops and capital letters. On a superficial view, this would be equated with repeatable observable performances of one or two narrowly specifiable kinds. Pupils write freely using full stops and capital letters appropriately, or they are able to punctuate prose passages provided for them in which capitals and full stops have been left out. Needless to say, much more than this would be needed if the pupil is subsequently to operate as an adult in a range of contexts. Someone producing copy in an advertising agency might be severely handicapped if unable to write sequences of words which did not conform to conventional punctuation. The same might go for a journalist writing headlines, the creator of tonight's takeaway menu written on a board outside the shop, or the secretary keying in entries to a database. Different qualities might be called for if the employee needed to correct the use of capitals and full stops in other people's written work. The literate milkman might recognise abuse of full stops and capitals in notes about milk from householders, but is likely to refrain from pointing this out to his customers.

I am not trying to imply by listing punctuation-relevant tasks that a person lacks the relevant 'ability' unless he can perform most or all of them. Indeed, later we will have reason to question the coherence of ability concepts of this kind. What the above examples are designed to show is that the punctuation competence concerned is far removed from a merely practical, observable piece of know-how or thin procedural skill. Anyone successful in at least a modest subset of these contexts will need a substantial element of declarative knowledge. The latter might include some grasp of the nature of sentences, incorporating awareness of grammatical structures. In addition there might be insight into the kinds of contexts in which properly punctuated prose is required, and in contrast those contexts when more 'informal' language use would be appropriate.

A substantial proportion of what constitutes literacy does appear to be made up of know-how suffused with declarative knowledge. Obvious examples include the skill of reading itself. Within literacy it may also be possible to identify other skills which are *prima facie* 'thin' and unsaturated with declarative knowledge. If I know how to spell 'diarrhoea', then I can spell it on demand, I write it correctly when creating my own prose, perhaps tell others the correct letters, and so forth. My competencies seem specifiable, straightforwardly observable, and relatively free from associated declarative knowledge. Other instances of a similar type might include being able to write legibly. Even these would still incorporate an element of, so to speak, 'thin' declarative knowledge, such as knowing that there are spaces between words, that English is written from left to right and from top to bottom, and so forth.

I have used without explanation a notion of 'thinness' in the context of declarative knowledge. Ultimately this will not prove to be a satisfactory level of treatment. For the moment, I can state that 'thin' declarative knowledge is comparatively isolated and unconnected with other items known. The issue of the 'connectedness' of knowledge deserves and will receive a full treatment later.

Within literacy there must be a good deal of 'deference', not so much to experts as to convention. My belief about the spelling of 'diarrhoea' can only be justified by appeal to linguistic convention. It is useful if I understand in general terms how this convention operates, the function of dictionaries, and how spellings sometimes come to change over time. Evidently the literate child will hardly have this much background.

I have said that in my judgement much of literacy's most central and significant content is 'rich'. The same point may be made equally forcefully in connection with numeracy. If we consider the 'capacity' to add numbers this appears to be a mixture of know-how suffused with rich declarative knowledge. The latter is 'rich' since someone with this capacity will know that addition is linked with subtraction, and know ways in which addition may be applied to money, length, time, etc.

An ability to use a calculator could not for very long be considered as a thin procedural skill; there were some brief observations about this in an earlier section. Knowing how to press keys to make numbers come up on the screen and knowing the order in which to press numbers, operator keys and the equals key to perform the four operations might seem 'thin', but only if these capacities are taken out of their proper context. Calculator users need to be able to estimate the likely magnitude of the answer in case wrong keys are pressed. They require a repertoire of sensible checking methods. These might include keying in additions in a different order and adding the answer of a subtraction calculation to the number subtracted to obtain the starting number. The user must understand which arithmetical operation(s) are required by a problem, and much more. All this implies a considerable weight of background declarative knowledge about the number system, place value, how number operations may be related to aspects of the real world, etc.

Mention was made above of the conventional element in literacy. My knowledge of writing includes many beliefs whose justification comes to an end with the arbitrary English spelling rules. Here, justification and understanding do not interrelate at a deeper level, since there is no deeper level for them to inhabit. This point does not hold good for all aspects of literacy. For example, declarative knowledge informing my use of punctuation when I enter items in a database certainly includes some knowledge of convention. But a good deal of it consists of knowledge of the function and purposes of databases, and how these relate to the appropriate deployment, for instance of capital letters and full stops. The relationship is largely dictated by the very nature of a database: given that we use databases for such and such purposes, then it is logical to use punctuation thus. The link here is largely not a matter of convention but of logic and reason. The declarative knowledge incorporated in my literacy which does not involve linguistic convention may well require me to hold beliefs whose justifications reach down deeply into the purposes and functions of language and much else.

There are certainly plenty of conventional elements within mathematics which to some extent mirror the conventional elements in written and spoken language. Symbols are used by agreement to mean specific operations or relationships. There are many technical terms and jargon phrases. Justified beliefs involved in numeracy include those concerning conventions of this kind. Other beliefs will be justified through an appreciation of the relationships which are the focus of the belief contents.

Now a pupil could have a justified belief that $8 + 7 = 15$ because his teacher has said so and his teacher has proved reliable on other matters, especially those of a mathematical character. Furthermore, it might well be expected that the numerate pupil will know many number facts of this kind 'by heart'; he will possess instant recall and will not need, for instance to count up on his fingers, or use an informal mental calculation method such as rounding 8 up to 10, and taking 2 of the 7, so adding 5 and making 15.

However, at the heart of numeracy, or so it may seem, should be a deeper understanding of numbers, their interrelationships and the meaning of arithmetical operations. It is this which should ground justifications of beliefs involved in knowing that $8 + 7 = 15$. The numerate person, it may be thought, does not simply possess a collection of number facts or rules 'without reason'. He understands why they must be so, or in the case of more complex content can construct from simpler elements, which are understood in this reasoned way, sound justifications or even 'proofs'. I understand that $\frac{1}{2}$ divided by $\frac{1}{4}$ is 2, and exactly why this is so, and further that $1\frac{1}{2}$ divided by $\frac{1}{4}$ is 6. From these simple cases, I see that 'turn upside down and multiply' is a rule which works for dividing fractions, and hence can proceed to use the same rule for examples such as $\frac{5}{16}$ divided by $\frac{1}{23}$. My justification for employing the same rule is sound, even though I cannot in this more complex case 'see' through to the way the fractions are related as I can in the simpler cases.

As I have already signalled, the fact that we can easily sketch this richer conception of numeracy does not imply that it forms a coherent psychological entity which pupils can definitively acquire.

The same point holds good of 'literacy'. I spend much time later in the book in the development of objections to the thought that these putative rich competencies might have a cohesive identity and coherence.

CONCLUSION

What has already been said about 'proper' knowledge and understanding has significant implications for the possibility of assessment and accountability. However we are not yet in a position to begin to explore these implications in real depth. Our investigation first requires a journey into crucial new territory. The issue of the connectedness of knowledge has already been mentioned, and linked to a characterisation of understanding. To tackle this issue properly, we need to look at a set of perspectives within philosophy of mind and language described as 'holist'. This will be the central topic of the next chapter.

NOTES AND REFERENCES

1. I will not attempt to spell out condition (4) in any detail. I do not know a way of doing so in an uncontroversial way, and even an attempt is likely to embroil me further in what has seemed to some to be a 'kind of private philosophical game, which is of no interest except to the players' (Dancy, J. (1985), *Introduction to Contemporary Epistemology* (Oxford, Blackwell)). Dancy discusses the 'irritating' cases stemming from E. L. Gettier (Gettier, E. (1963), Is justified true belief knowledge? *Analysis* 23, pp. 121–123) which show that the first three conditions for knowing are not in themselves sufficient for knowledge. He feels that they involve inference from a false but justified belief to a further justified belief which happens to be true. Gettier's examples have provoked an immense yet abstruse literature which is very much 'philosophers' philosophy'. I refer the interested reader to Dancy, as further consideration of this issue is not part of the philosophical framework within which I am going to examine educational assessment.

Chapter 3
Understanding and Holism

In the last chapter a conception of 'rich' or 'proper' knowledge was sketched. For discussion purposes it was stipulated as understood knowledge. I made it clear that these moves should in no way be thought to settle fundamental questions about how, if at all, we can make *identifying reference* to such knowledge. We must return to these questions in Chapter 6.

I have claimed that if someone understands something which they know, this is at least partly in virtue of their appropriately connecting it to other knowledge which they also possess. This chapter discusses at some length the notion of *knowledge connectedness*, since it has fundamental implications for the extent to which it is possible to assess 'proper' knowledge. It is almost impossible to capture the elusive yet crucial idea of *connectedness* in literal terms. Yet a failure to understand its meaning and significance underlies much unwarranted optimism about the potential accuracy of educational assessment. Later we shall be in a position to subject this optimism to critical scrutiny.

A variety of perspectives developed within analytical philosophy this century are referred to as 'holist'. We can gain some insights into *connectedness* by having recourse to these perspectives. Several distinct notions of holism receive considerable support from modern analytical philosophers. I will not assume that to embrace one holism is to embrace them all.

In this chapter I discuss in turn property holism, holism about propositions and content, meaning holism, belief and concept holisms and anthropological holism, and I proceed to locate Richard Skemp's distinction between instrumental and relational understanding within these holist doctrines. I will argue that with the exception of meaning holism there is much to be said for all these versions. Once they have been explained in some detail, they can support a richer interpretation of the 'connectedness' of understood knowledge than has been possible so far in my discussion. This extended discussion of holisms will play a fundamental role in realising the aim of this book, which is to comprehend the limits of the educational assessment of understood knowledge. These implications are discussed in Chapter 5, and again in the treatment of matching given in Chapter 7. I hope that the importance of the topic will be seen to justify the technical nature of some of the argument.

Fodor and Lepore (1992) provide a stimulating if hostile review of contemporary holisms. In the following sections I take some liberties with their treatment, turning their discussions to my own purposes. I do not claim to represent their views accurately, nor do I commit myself to agreeing with any of their opinions of the positions they discuss.

PROPERTY HOLISM

Properties are invariably related to other properties. The relationship between them may be as close as mutual logical implication. For instance, having shape entails having size, and vice versa. Often the link cannot be characterised in formal logical terms, yet is still fundamental. The nature of being a bank is closely tied to that of being money, and to what it is to be a borrower or a lender of money. It is difficult to explain this connection except by saying that bankhood cannot be what it is without its relationship to the property of being money or the equivalent. Incidentally, stating such relationships does not entail that the properties are actually instantiated. The kinds of links to which I refer *obtain comprehensively between properties of all kinds*. They should not be confused with specific connections which exist between *relational* properties such as being a father and being a son.

This way of speaking raises the question of how, if at all, properties can be *counted*. How can it be decided whether just one property is under consideration, or more than one? Do such questions even make sense? It is a familiar point in analytical philosophy that we lack defensible identity criteria for properties. The meaning of predicate P may differ from that of Q, but it does not follow from this that distinct properties are attributed to subjects through the use of these predicates. Moreover is it clear that *sameness* of predicate meaning guarantees that the same property is attributed each time? Familiar examples provoke characteristic difficulties. Consider the following.

'The blade is keen' may be compared with 'Her mind is keen'. It is plausible to claim that 'is keen' has the same *meaning* in each of these sentences. Judgement on this issue may in part be determined by whether the second occurrence of the predicate is thought to be metaphorical, and whether the favoured theory of metaphor involves shifts of *meaning* in the transformation from literal to metaphorical use of the 'same' predicate.

If we put metaphor theory to one side and consider the matter directly, common sense suggests that 'is keen' attributes a different *property* to a mind from that which it attributes to a knife blade. If we say this, should we also now claim that the meaning of 'is keen' when applied to minds differs from 'is keen' when applied to knives? Or can predicates retain a particular meaning even when they are used to assign different properties?

Even if sameness of predicate meaning could plausibly be put forward as a significant indicator of property identity, it only shifts the problem to finding criteria for synonymy. Now despite Quine (1953) it might be argued that the unavailability of criteria for synonymy does not entail that synonymy itself is a wholly defective concept. Nevertheless, the unavailability of criteria for synonymy is peculiarly unhelpful if attempts are going to be made to cite sameness or difference of predicate meaning in support of judgements about property identity.

It may be argued that these intractable problems are a symptom of the fact that holism about properties is true. To sum up the doctrine I want to defend here, the notion of a discrete, stand-alone property is wholly unintelligible. Properties exist in connected clusters. I now spend a few paragraphs developing this claim, first focusing on why anyone might have thought otherwise.

Property discourse does give the impression that we can consider just one property at a time, or that in contrast we can refer to a collection of several, made up from individual identifiable properties. Language enables us to invent terms such as 'the attribute of blueness' or 'the property of being a chair' which apparently refer to particular properties just as 'the table in the corner' may be used to pick out a particular table. It may not seem obviously perverse in the first instance to interpret the function of a predicate expression such as 'is a chair' in 'That wooden object is a chair' as attributing a particular property to the said wooden object.

I can refer to the various chairs in my room, one by one. They are distinguishable from each other, and each possesses independent existence. I could have just one of them in my room at any time. Now it may seem possible to imagine properties having an existence which at least in some ways parallels the status of physical objects which I have just mentioned. On such a perspective it may be thought that we can refer to single properties just as we can refer to single physical objects. Even if the obvious point is granted that there are necessary connections between different properties, such as having shape and having size, or being red and being coloured, it still may appear that distinct independent items are being said to be necessarily connected in this way.

I would argue that on closer scrutiny this impression of distinctness often proves illusory. The comparison with physical objects is much more misleading than we think. We can make the first moves towards understanding the differences between the status of physical objects and of properties easily enough. For instance, properties possess an intrinsically 'general' character. Yet language may still beguile us into discerning non-existent resemblances between the status of physical objects and of properties. Study of one or two examples is a good way of escaping from the spell.

No one would dispute that the property of being grass is 'connected' with the property of being alive and the property of being something that grows. These particular connections are not logically necessary. Being grass does not logically imply being something that grows, otherwise dead grass would be an impossibility. (It may logically imply being something that grows at some time or other, but that is different.) Nevertheless the very nature of what it is to be grass is bound up with what it is to grow and what it is to be alive.

I am not trying to paint a picture here of separate atomistic properties chained together. *Being grass* is not wholly distinct and separable from *being a growing thing*. In attributing what may appear to be separable distinct properties, we are actually indicating various aspects of a more global situation or 'whole'. Sometimes the term 'network' is used in this regard, and later I will employ it myself. However, the danger of this further metaphor is that we still may imagine discrete items which are connected in the network.

An example which is helpful in bringing out the way in which properties can be 'linked', and the way in which they do not possess discrete identities of their own, is the property of having a position in space and time. Position subsists in virtue of relationships to other positions in space and time. All positions are related to each other. A particular position cannot exist in complete isolation from other positions. The notion is unintelligible.

Consider two more analogies. The strength of my queen's position on the chess board is not something that makes any sense considered on its own. Its very essence derives from its relationships to my other pieces, and to my opponent's pieces. The function of the liver makes essential reference to functions of other bodily organs and processes. Its purpose inextricably involves aspects of what is happening elsewhere in the body.

This notion of 'intrinsic connection' is admittedly hard to explain in other terms. It does not, however, cover precisely the same relationships as 'logically necessary connection'. Some properties between which there exists a logically necessary link are not 'intrinsically connected' in the sense I am trying to discuss. For instance, in mathematics it is possible through extensive and elaborate proofs to establish logical implications between properties which are very 'distant' from each other. On the other hand, some properties between which there do seem to be intrinsic connections are not directly linked by logically necessary ties, as in the *being grass* and *being a growing thing* example.

In the term 'distance' there is yet another metaphor, which I also use later in connection with other types of holism. I have discussed this metaphor before (Davis, 1995) and suggested that, for example, the topic of ice cream is very 'distant' from the topic of galaxies. The meaning of such a claim has a certain intuitive obviousness, though attempts to say much more about it soon founder. A list of galaxy properties, and other properties to which galaxy properties are connected, would be unlikely to include any ice cream properties.

Within mathematics some topics are further apart than others, and hence the possibility of surprise when distant properties are established to be necessarily connected. However, 'surprise' has an epistemological flavour, and we should be careful not to suggest that it could be used as a criterion of the 'distance' between properties. In an earlier paper I hinted that objective criteria for judging distance might be unavailable in principle. 'Judgements about distance may be essentially bound up with the particular purposes and values of those making the judgements' (Davis, 1995).

Neither the concept of 'distance' nor that of 'intrinsic connection' then may be rigorously defined, nor supplied with clear criteria for their application. I do not believe that this undermines the coherence or the importance of the points just made about the ways in which properties are connected. In some ways the situation resembles the status of the concept of synonymy. There is no consensus about *criteria* for application of the term 'has the same meaning as', but in practice the term is important and useful. Grice and Strawson came to a similar conclusion many years ago (Grice and Strawson, 1956).

Again in the article mentioned I explored the thought in connection with belief holism that some beliefs do possess or should possess higher degrees of interconnectedness than others. A similar point may be made about properties. The property of having such and such a mass is interconnected with other properties involved in Newtonian mechanics, such as requiring a given force to achieve a given acceleration. Newtonian properties are explicitly constructed in terms of each other. Consider also an example of a property which behaves differently from Newtonian properties, namely the property of having an average temperature of 29.1°F in January. This *is* connected with calendar issues, number properties, temperature, and so on. However it is not connected (unless climatologists are able to establish loose empirical connections) with properties to do with average temperatures in other months. Properties of having such and such monthly average temperatures are, so to speak, locally isolated from each other.

HOLISM ABOUT PROPOSITIONS AND CONTENT

Many of the themes in property holism reappear when we examine propositions and content. 'Proposition' is a philosopher's term of art, and a rather old-fashioned one at that. Analytical philosophy has conducted complex debates in the past about whether and in what sense propositions 'exist', and about identity criteria for propositions. It is fair to say that no conclusion has been established, and that many have decided that propositions are dubious entities just because firm identity criteria cannot be convincingly defended. Fortunately I think there is no necessity for a sophisticated position about these issues, as it does not affect the thrust of my argument. I do need a term for the topic of this section, which I hope I can use with impunity in a relatively informal way. So I intend to employ the term 'proposition' to cover the content which seems to be common to the following examples:

Jones believes that the bull will attack him
Jones fears that the bull will attack him
Jones would like the bull to attack him
Jones hopes that the bull will attack him
— and so forth.

I have made it easy by using the same form of words in these instances of propositional attitudes; most people would agree at least informally that there is some kind of content or proposition common to the four quoted. Up to a limited point, I could alter the wording after the main verb while still retaining agreement that the same content was present. After alterations have proceeded beyond a certain stage, disputes would arise about whether the 'same' proposition or content is involved.

As with properties, the fact that we can apparently pick out 'propositions' or content by using specific sequences of words may seem to suggest the possibility of discrete abstract entities: the proposition that Faraday discovered the dynamo, the proposition that Wittgenstein liked Westerns. Attempts at producing identity criteria for propositions have tried to determine how different word sequences might refer to the same object and say the 'same thing' about it. Discussions of the latter had to develop criteria for property identity, or, more specifically, to try to set out just when different (linguistic) predicates were assigning the 'same' property. The reason for this kind of approach to identity criteria for propositions is presumably roughly as follows. In an informal fashion, we do count as expressing the same proposition sentences which may differ substantially in their verbal form, but which pick out the same object and attribute the same property to it. It has not proved possible to codify this informal thinking. Insofar as it is coherent, it helps to show that whatever else they might be, propositions cannot be discrete and specifically identifiable items, since properties are not.

The proposition that Faraday discovered the dynamo is not wholly distinct from the proposition that a famous Victorian scientist whose first name was Michael discovered a mechanical means of generating direct current. It may be partially yet not entirely distinct from the proposition that the dynamo incorporates magnets and coils of wire, that the flow of current through a wire produces a magnetic field, and so on. That Faraday discovered the dynamo is not a 'stand alone' entity. Its essential nature is inextricably bound up with other propositions. (All the propositions just mentioned are of course true, but the same point usually holds for false or fictional propositions.)

I would not wish to defend a holism about propositions which implies that the same degree of 'connectivity' exists between all propositions. Further, the idea of 'distance' applies here as much as with properties. I am not able to justify further the claims just made about propositions being 'partially distinct' from each other or 'wholly distinct' from each other. Clear objective criteria for sameness or distinctness are not to be had here. I can only appeal to intuitions, and accept that on occasion yours may not be the same as mine.

MEANING HOLISM

I think holism about content, propositions, beliefs, concepts etc. in various senses is true and has significant implications for assessment. These implications will be explored later, especially in Chapters 5 and 7. I do not intend to say very much about meaning holism partly because I believe it is not germane to the main thrust of the argument in this book about assessment, and partly because I am not sure that versions known to me are even true. I comment on it briefly here if only to shed more light on the other kinds of holism with which I will be more concerned.

It might be said that an individual word or linguistic symbol has no meaning on its own, but only insofar as it has a role in language. That represents a rather extreme and general form of meaning holism. A more modest and focused version could be that words only have meaning within sentences, or paragraphs, and that these clusters of meaning should not be thought of as collections of semantic atoms. Either languages as wholes, or substantial sections of languages, possess meaning, which cannot be dissected into semantic atoms possessed by words.

There do seem to be some symbol systems of which meaning holism is true. '+' has no meaning in isolation, but only within a symbol system which also includes at least the natural numbers, a symbol such as '=' and so on.

Fodor and Lepore cite Michael Dummett as providing a powerful objection to meaning holism for natural languages, at least in any strong or global guise. Dummett (1973) argues that we could not communicate, nor could we even acquire language, were strong meaning holism true. As I understand him, the following represents the core of his complaint.

You can understand my sentence, which may be of a type an utterance of which you have never heard before, and I have never produced before. This possibility rests on the fact that we in some sense share a common understanding of common meanings possessed by the constituents of the sentence. This seems to imply that constituents or words can possess atomistic meanings. A particular word has a specific meaning, regardless of the meaning of any sentence of which it may be a part. This explains how sentences never encountered or uttered previously can nevertheless possess a meaning which is immediately understood. Further, if strong meaning holism were true, it would be very difficult to understand how language learning could ever begin. The young child would be unable to build up her knowledge of meanings bit by bit. She could not understand the meaning of a particular word before she grasped the meaning of many others. 'But then how, save in a single spasm of seamless cognition, could any language ever be learned?' (Fodor and Lepore, 1992).

Without pronouncing definitively on the strength of this objection, it is important to see how it does not also constitute a difficulty for holisms of other kinds. Consider the parallel issue of how children build up knowledge of properties. The child has only an attenuated grasp of the property of being a king on first encountering it. Her conception of kingship will gradually become fuller and richer as she understands associated properties, and how they connect with being a king. She can talk with adults about matters which she does not fully understand. Adults working with children have many opportunities to engage in conversations of this kind. A common language makes it possible. While we are far from understanding fully how this is achieved, there does not seem any obvious objection to property holism arising from this situation which would correspond to Dummett's objection to meaning holism. A child could not obtain a proper grasp of a given property without also appreciating the character of others. But there seems to be no reason to insist that the child must obtain a full understanding of a property all at once.

BELIEF AND CONCEPT HOLISMS

These introduce new considerations, since epistemological and psychological perspectives are essentially involved. At the same time, some of the arguments for belief holism spring from holism about propositions.

If the proposition that Faraday discovered the dynamo cannot be separated from other propositions about dynamos, electricity, coils, magnetic fields, the Victorian era, etc., then it may seem that someone cannot believe that Faraday discovered the dynamo without believing some of these other things too. While there is some substance in this thought, it must be treated with care.

First, there is a formal point. If Jones believes that p, and p logically entails q, it does not follow that Jones believes that q. If in this example logical entailment between p and q is replaced by other kinds of links or connections the same point can be made. Indeed, some argue that it is possible for Jones to believe both p and not p at one and the same time. Such argument would require an account of belief which made it quite clear how it was not to be identified with conscious feelings of conviction. The account is needed since it is very difficult to see how any *sane* person could consciously assent both to p and to *not p* at any one time. Questions might be raised about the extent to which insane people can have fully-fledged beliefs. Much more will need to be said about belief in general in the next chapter.

None of this prevents particular cases being made about what people 'must' believe when the content of one belief has a very intimate connection with that of another. If I believe that the Victorian scientist Faraday discovered the dynamo then arguably I must believe that dynamos had not already been invented by the time Faraday bent his scientific mind to the problem. There are many other beliefs I would also require. The argument here begins to touch on what could possibly count as believing that Faraday discovered the dynamo unless certain other beliefs are also present.

To take the discussion further we need to return to a consideration of the conditions in which it is appropriate to report someone else as having a particular belief. In Chapter 2 we began to look at this issue but specifically in relation to reports of someone's knowledge. Since knowledge entails belief, the discussion about reporting beliefs is to some extent parallel.

In a science lesson, copper is heated strongly, and turns black. It is weighed before and after the heating, and its mass is slightly greater afterwards. Pupils witness this experiment demonstrated by the teacher, and the question arises as to what they believe has happened. Now the teacher explains to the pupils that heating the copper caused it to combine with oxygen, that the black substance is an oxide of copper, and that the extra mass is oxygen. The teacher's explanation might be beautifully lucid. Yet its effect upon the beliefs of a typical pupil, John, might be modest in the short term. The teacher hopes that he believes that the copper oxidised on heating. However, she might be wise to confine her assessment of John's belief to terms which closely reflect how in all likelihood John thinks of the event in question. Perhaps John's opinion at this point is simply that heating the copper caused it to become heavier. The teacher is likely to hope that her explanations made more impact than that suggested by this version of John's opinion. However, she must be careful not to 'spread' without justification the notions she would use to conceptualise the copper event, into her interpretation of what is in John's mind.

Jane might hold that the Evening Star is brighter than Sirius. Though astronomically advanced for her age, she does not know that the Evening Star is in fact the planet Venus. She would therefore not allow that she believed that Venus is brighter than Sirius. Nevertheless, there might be circumstances in which it was convenient or appropriate to report her as believing that Venus is brighter than Sirius. This could happen even if those reporting her belief were quite clear about the limitations of her astronomical knowledge.

There has been a great deal of complex discussion about the supposedly related issue of *de dicto* and *de re* beliefs. We will try to avoid much in the way of abstruse technicalities, but some of the issues here are fundamental to our inquiries into assessment. I have argued (Davis, 1986), following Searle (1980), that we do not have different kinds of beliefs here, but a range of styles in which beliefs are reported. I may comment on Jane's state of mind, concentrating, so to speak, on what I think is in her head, in which case I will not say she believes that Venus is brighter than Sirius. To use the traditional term, my report is *de dicto*. Alternatively I may choose in my observation to speak both of Jane's psychological state and of the world in which she is situated (at least as I believe it to be) and to report her as believing that Venus is brighter than Sirius. Then my report is *de re*. I am saying that Venus is believed by Jane to be brighter than Sirius. In more complicated belief reports, hybrids of *de re* and *de dicto* report may occur.

For the time being, let us accept the distinction between on the one hand 'what is in someone's mind' and on the other hand, the nature of the world external to that mind and how it relates to that mind. I do not wish to assume that this distinction is the *same* as that between *de dicto* and *de re* belief reports, even if the latter distinction is still felt to be acceptable. This is because there seem to be a range of ways in which my report of someone's belief may take into account matters other than 'the contents of their mind'. To employ a referring expression whose referent is certainly an item about which the belief is held, yet where the said referring expression would not be deemed applicable by the believer, represents just one possibility. Other modes of incorporating more than what is thought to be in the believer's head include references to concepts and properties to which their belief seems to be related, but whose full import and range of other connections is not felt to be grasped by the believer.

Causal theories of reference, fashionable in the 1970s and 1980s, spawned plenty of plausible examples. Natural kind terms such as 'gold', 'water' or 'oak' were held to be involved in a division of linguistic labour (Putnam, 1977). On this account, chemists have a full understanding of 'gold' or 'water' involving a grasp of their place in current well-confirmed scientific theories and of connections with other knowledge in chemistry and physics. The layman may have little or no grasp of this. Nevertheless he or she can still use the terms perfectly adequately, communicate reference and meaning and form relevant propositional attitudes. For instance, he can hold fully-fledged 'gold beliefs'. One chemist can report to another chemist that a lay person has a belief about gold. The chemists' shared 'gold understanding' is far richer than that of the lay person. It is perfectly appropriate to report the lay belief as being about gold in the full scientific sense. Yet this report as understood by the chemists incorporates many aspects of gold which are certainly not 'in the lay person's head'. Indeed if the chemists are pressed on the matter they might well concede that they had not meant to imply that the lay person has as much in his head about gold as the chemists themselves.

We are trying to focus at present on interpretations of another person, in which we are concentrating on her state of mind. We are concerned with how *she* takes things to be. In the course of such interpretations, it is being argued that we are unable to make sense of an interpretation that someone has a particular belief which brings no other beliefs in its train. In interpreting someone as believing X we are in effect understanding her as possessing an indefinite but substantial 'number' of beliefs. The word 'number' is in scare quotes because, of course, we have no clear way of counting beliefs. It would be impossible to indicate clearly the extent of the belief system required; we can only gesture at the areas to be covered. Holists about belief generally add what are sometimes referred to as 'principles of charity', for instance 'Maximise the coherence of the beliefs ascribed and maximise the truth of the beliefs ascribed (both from the ascriber's point of view, of course, and both *ceteris paribus*)' (Fodor and Lepore, 1992).

The case discussed earlier of the child being told something authoritatively by her aunt may appear to be a counter-example. The child apparently possesses a belief which can stand by itself.

However, we need to be careful about the detail here. What of the extreme case? The child told that colourless green ideas sleep furiously does not actually believe this. First and foremost, she does not believe it because there is nothing to believe. Even if there were, the best that could be said would be that the child believes that her aunt has conveyed a truth to her, and can employ a form of words in which to report it. She does not know what she is reporting. To believe something, she must have at least some understanding of its purported content.

If we move away from the absurdity of the Chomskyan example, and change the case by making the aunt produce a sentence of which the child has some grasp, we are automatically discounting the possibility of an atomic belief. Even rudimentary content will come in substantial interconnected networks, so to speak, rather than isolated elements.

Some readers will need little more in the way of hints to appreciate that the discussion of this chapter so far already has important implications for assessment. However, a more explicit discussion of these themes will have to wait for later chapters. The points about the way we report beliefs, and the impossibility of conceptualising beliefs as discrete, stand-alone items will prove particularly significant.

It might be thought that, at least for language speakers, if a speaker sincerely utters a statement in appropriate or normal circumstances, we can unhesitatingly attribute a specific belief to him. This is without regard to any other beliefs he might or might not hold. The content of his belief is indicated by the statement which is made. It may be argued that this line of thinking damages claims for holism about beliefs.

Leaving aside any difficulties in making clear what 'appropriate' or 'normal' is to mean, there are well-known objections to this line of thought. When we attribute a belief to a speaker on the basis of his utterance of a particular sentence we must at the same time be attributing to him beliefs about the meaning of that sentence.

For instance, suppose it is thought that that an utterance of 'Faraday discovered the dynamo' can provide us with a paradigm case of belief with a specific content. Now precisely which belief would this be? The answer depends on, among other things, the meanings the speaker attaches to 'Faraday', 'discovered' and 'dynamo'. If she thinks that 'dynamo' means 'small solar-powered generator', then her belief is false. The belief in question would be different from the belief concerned if she thought that a dynamo was a device for generating electricity by moving magnets and coils of wire in relation to each other.

It is trivially true that whether a speaker uses a particular sentence to express her belief depends on what she thinks the sentence means.

Our quest for precise identification of a belief 'atom' by means of utterances founders when we appreciate what else the speaker might need to believe in order to have the relevant thoughts about the meanings of the terms in her sentence. She cannot have any sensible thoughts about the meaning of 'dynamo' without a reasonably extensive network of connected beliefs about electricity, etc. The same holistic comments can be made here as we made earlier about belief in general.

So far we have considered belief holism in relation to cognitive content. Philosophers such as David Lewis, Donald Davidson and others have made a wider holism about our interpretations of the behaviour and language of others very familiar (e.g. Lewis, 1974; Davidson, 1973; Davidson, 1974).

When I judge that Jones believes that the bull will attack him, I observe his behaviour, and what, if anything, he is saying. I note the environment in which he is situated. On the basis of all this, I perform a complex act of interpretation, part of which is the attribution of the said belief. Not only will I need to attribute a range of beliefs to him, but also I will need to make assumptions about his desires and intentions. I see him running away from a bull, which is pawing the ground angrily. If on the basis of this I conclude that he believes the bull will attack him, I am also assuming at least some of the following:

He believes bulls are dangerous;
He does not want dangerous animals attacking him;
He believes that the bull pawing the ground is a prelude to charging after him;
He intends to escape the effects of the likely charge;
He has no other intention which takes priority over escaping, e.g. to practise some bull-fighting manoeuvres before he visits Spain.

These assumptions seem quite unexceptional. If he was in a suicidal state of mind, suspected that if he continued to stand quietly the bull would not attack, and judged that running away from the bull would encourage it to pursue him, this would also 'explain' his behaviour. The 'natural' interpretation, that he is running away because he believes the bull will attack him, is one of an indefinite number of possible interpretations. A 'whole' interlocking picture of beliefs, desires and intentions has to be attributed to Jones, viewed as an active conscious agent within a particular context. Given all this, one specific belief-attribution seems to make the most sense in folk-psychological terms. That is to say that we make judgements according to our theories of what motivates people to act and to speak, and about their likely hopes and fears.

Platitudinous though much of this material may seem when not wrapped up in philosophical terminology, it has profound implications for the true potential of certain kinds of educational assessment. By the end of the next chapter it will be apparent that the judgement that someone believes that *p* cannot be a claim that they are in a specific state in virtue of which they hold the particular belief in question. Belief attributions are in contrast looser, and not such as to be unambiguously true or false. Attempts to assess pupils often seems to assume otherwise.

ANTHROPOLOGICAL HOLISM

I take this term from Fodor and Lepore (1992), without wholly endorsing the use they make of it. Wittgenstein, Austin and others argued that the meaning of a term was constituted by its role in a system of beliefs, practices, institutions, conventions, culture and rituals. Language considered away from the practices in which it is embedded is language on holiday. The 'holism' of this perspective ties meanings to beliefs and practices, suggesting that they are interrelated, and that there is a fundamental sense in which the interrelations do not obtain between distinct items.

Later we will look at the way in which knowledge claims and abilities are themselves only identifiable within contexts of beliefs, practices and culture. We examine the insights of writers in the 'situated cognition' tradition as regards this issue, and the extent to which it is a philosophical rather than an anthropological insight. The implications for educational assessment will then be developed.

RICHARD SKEMP'S COGNITIVE MAPS, AND THE RELATIONAL/INSTRUMENTAL UNDERSTANDING DISTINCTION

Richard Skemp's (1989) classic distinction between relational and instrumental understanding makes use of some 'holist' metaphors, although the term holism does not appear in his writing to my knowledge. In order to make the distinction, he draws on an analogy with maps. He compares and contrasts the position of two people attempting to make their way to a venue, e.g. a church in an unknown town. Each has a series of direction: 'Left, under the railway bridge, right, left, and the church is ahead of you'. The first person does not have a map. If he goes wrong in following the sequence he is lost, and will only find his way by sheer luck. The second person has a map. If he deviates from the directions sequence, he can locate himself on the map, and find his way either back to the sequence, or he can devise himself a new route.

The position of someone without a map is likened to the mastery of a person in possession of rules, or 'thin' knowledge of facts 'without reason'. He may apply these rules inappropriately, since he lacks an understanding and justification for them. If he forgets the rule, he cannot reconstruct it, and he cannot devise an alternative way of solving the problem. The individual 'only' has instrumental understanding. The map owner, on the other hand, can reconstruct a rule if he forgets all or part of it. He can devise new ways of solving the problem altogether if necessary. He possesses relational understanding. The growth of relational understanding consists of the learner constructing an increasing number of routes from one 'place' to another.

The image of a cognitive map suggests concepts connected by routes, and suggests too that the person in possession of a good cognitive map is able to make all kinds of different connections. Skemp does not seem to be a fully-fledged, explicit holist about concepts. He does not, for instance, say that a given concept would not be what it is without its connections to other concepts. It is his focus on routes or connections which is relevant to the context of holisms. And while he is discussing mathematics, the issues he raises have much wider implications. He acknowledges the difficulty of teaching relational understanding, and under the heading 'Difficulty of assessment of whether a person understands relationally or instrumentally' he observes: 'From the marks he makes on paper, it is very hard to make valid inference about the mental processes by which a pupil has been led to make them' (Skemp, 1989 p. 13). In the light of the arguments I am trying to develop in this book, the phrase 'very hard' should be changed for 'sometimes impossible in principle'.

It is not clear that Skemp would wish to distinguish between declarative knowledge and 'knowing how'. While acknowledging the roughness of the distinction, I am assuming for the sake of this discussion that Skemp's observations are relevant to the nature of understanding incorporated into declarative knowledge. I have suggested (Davis, 1995) that his division between relational and instrumental understanding might be regarded as cutting across or blurring two sets of contrasts: one between knowledge which I can 'substantially' justify without deference to authority and knowledge which I mainly justify by deference to authority, and a second between knowledge of which I have little understanding and knowledge of which I have a deep understanding.

We saw earlier that justified beliefs involving little or no deference to the expertise of others require understanding, but acknowledged that some propositions I thoroughly understand I may not be justified in believing. Skemp claims to be distinguishing between kinds of understanding; he is also in effect drawing a contrast between types of justification. This is perhaps not surprising. As a maths educationist Skemp is unlikely to take much interest in knowledge involving significant deference to others' expertise. Pupils with mathematical knowledge are supposed to be able to understand and to justify it for themselves.

Relational understanding is thought somehow to feature a grasp of the routes between propositions and concepts, or an appreciation of the relationships and connections between 'different' kinds of content. It is tempting to make a simple identification of the kind of understanding required for 'proper' knowledge with Skemp's 'relational' understanding. However, in mathematics we have already seen that there is a special possibility of restricted understanding: someone might have a good relational understanding within pure mathematics itself, without the capacity to use and apply it to the real world. The interconnections between concepts grasped in respect of this particular type of relational understanding could all be inside mathematics, viewed as an abstract uninterpreted system.

However, relational understanding of mathematics as interpretable or applicable to the world must include a grasp of 'connections' between abstract mathematical concepts and empirical concepts. Admittedly yet more knowledge than this may be needed for use and application: the wide range of ideas covered under the heading 'using and applying' explored in Chapter 2 certainly included some involving substantial 'know-how'.

Pure mathematics aside, we can agree that 'relational' understanding in other subjects is what is required for proper knowledge. It certainly seems to fit the requirements of literacy and numeracy examined in Chapter 2.

CONCLUSION

The survey of holisms, and the locating of Richard Skemp's instrumental and relational understanding within the 'holist landscape', has illuminated the idea of the connectedness of understood knowledge. The true beliefs which knowledge involves cannot be attributed to an agent without also attributing other beliefs to that agent. The content of a 'single' belief is not intelligible in itself, but only 'exists' in its connections and relationships to other content. Properties themselves, known to be possessed by objects, require other properties to 'support' them. If my knowledge is 'proper' or 'rich' and hence understood, I have a grip on the way the content, propositions and properties concerned are appropriately connected to much else in the way of content, propositions and properties.

In order to mount the principled critique of educational assessment, a fair amount of philosophical scene-setting is necessary. I am styling much of the knowledge involved in literacy and numeracy of interest to a modern economy as 'proper' or 'rich', and we have needed to spend some time reflecting on what this might mean. At the heart of the explanation lie issues of connectedness, and of use and application. Connectedness is being put forward as a necessary condition for understanding. It may also be argued that it is a necessary condition for use and application. A piece of knowledge unconnected to other knowledge in the mind of the knower evidently cannot be used and applied in a variety of circumstances. However, connectedness is not a sufficient condition for use and application, since the latter may often involve practical 'know-how'.

The scene-setting continues as we now turn our attention more generally to the concept of belief. I have written about this topic before (Davis, 1986) and draw on that paper in the following chapter, while developing significantly my earlier argument. When this discussion is complete we will be ready to bring together what has been said about knowledge, belief, understanding, and use and application, and make a direct examination of the implications for educational assessment practices.

Chapter 4
Belief and Language-based Assessment

In this chapter an account of belief is defended which might be referred to as a 'loose functional theory'. On a common-sense perspective, it may seem that when an agent possesses a particular belief he or she is in a specific identifiable discrete state, and that it is perfectly possible for a third party to discover whether or not that agent possesses the said belief. Some such 'realist' perspective is required if it is assumed that language produced by that agent, whether written or spoken, provides a peculiarly effective and unambiguous manifestation of the 'fact' that the agent possesses the belief in question. However, in what follows I contend that this common-sense perspective does not offer valid insights into the nature of belief. It is argued on the contrary that beliefs are not discrete items whose existence can be detected 'within the heads' of agents. Evidently this 'anti-realist' account of belief has profound implications for the viability of a range of current practices in educational assessment. Some of these implications are explored in the discussions which immediately follow in Chapter 5, while others must await treatment in later sections, including the examination of matching in Chapter 7. This chapter begins by making some brief observations on the educational background to the dominance of language-based assessment and the assumption that specific pupil beliefs may be readily detected by means of such assessment. It proceeds to rehearse objections to traditional 'propositional' theories of belief of the kind which are required to support 'realist' notions of belief as specific states whose presence may be manifested by an agent's use of language. In the light of these objections, it outlines a looser, anti-realist account of belief.

In the UK in the late 1970s and early 1980s the government set up a system for assessing the performance levels of large samples of pupils at various ages in basic school subjects. The body responsible for this was known as the Assessment of Performance Unit, or APU. It was maintained by the APU, and by the creators of the early National Curriculum Standard Assessment Tasks (SATs), that assessment can neither be effective nor comprehensive if it is restricted to evidence from pupils in the form of their written or spoken language.

The complaint that written products are over-used in the business of assessing educational achievement is familiar. A combination of written plus oral evidence and information about other aspects of pupil behaviour is held by some assessment experts to be 'better'. That is to say, a wider selection of evidence is thought to enable us to make *more accurate*, or *truer*, judgements about current attainment.

It is of course convenient, less time consuming and usually cheaper to focus on the written or spoken word. The SATs in England and Wales have gradually become distanced from the original Task Group on Assessment and Testing ideal. This was that at least at the primary age practical activities should be used in addition to written tests for assessment purposes. Public examinations for secondary pupils are still dominated by controlled events in which pupils produce written responses to order.

Concentrating on language-based assessment may contribute to the illusion that it is possible to pinpoint a pupil's current knowledge state with reasonable accuracy, and hence that a tight match of task to pupil is feasible. It may help to support the dogma that pupil learning outcomes can be assessed sufficiently effectively to enable schools to be held accountable for their 'products' in a tough-minded fashion.

Experienced infant teachers are especially likely to be aware of the problems associated with an overuse of language for assessment. They will, of course, talk to their pupils in an effort to discover what they believe and understand. Nevertheless, they will have strong convictions that their pupils may hold beliefs which they cannot articulate, especially in mathematics and science (Davis, 1986).

For example, a child is trying to make a LOGO-driven turtle go away from him, to travel round a pile of bricks and return to its starting point. He chooses the wrong angle when the return journey commences. The turtle begins to travel sideways, and not towards him at all. Hastily the angle is 'corrected' by the child in the next command. Perhaps the child can say something about this when asked. Perhaps not. In view of the deliberate, conscious way in which he makes the correction he might be characterised as believing something about the angles concerned even though he is unable to express his thinking on the matter.

Or again (Davis, 1986), a child is building with wooden bricks. She wants a brick to stick out horizontally from a wall, to form part of the roof of her structure. She does not want to place the horizontal brick with half sticking out on one side and half sticking out on the other: this would be untidy, and provide insufficient roofing. Yet were the horizontal brick to be placed precisely as she wishes, the structure would fail to balance. Quite deliberately, she selects a small heavy block, and puts it on top of the horizontal brick in a vertical line with the wall. Her horizontal brick can now be made to stick out in the way she desires, and is reasonably stable. Perhaps she cannot say anything about why she does this. Yet might she not be characterised as having beliefs concerning fulcrums? Could this not be a reasonable step even if we are careful to bear in mind the distinction between different ways of reporting beliefs which were mentioned in the last chapter?

To provide the philosophical background to claims about the limitations of language-based assessment we need access to an appropriate theory of belief. As we will see, such a theory also helps us to achieve a more comprehensive view of the inherent weaknesses of much educational assessment based on limited samples of pupil language and behaviour. These weaknesses afflict all attempts to assess knowledge, understanding and skill richer than the 'thinnest' procedural competence.

Such matters are tackled directly in the following chapter, and the theme is pursued further in the chapters on transfer, matching, and the validity and reliability of criterion-referenced assessment systems. Our next task is to consider argument for an appropriate theory of belief.

BELIEF THEORY

If I learn that Faraday discovered the dynamo, then there was a time when I did not know this. When I learn that Faraday discovered the dynamo I come to know it. This does not rule out the possibility that there might on occasion be more to learning than coming to know. I want to concentrate for the moment on the implications of my being in possession of the relevant knowledge. Let us assume that the orthodox conditions for knowing that *p* quoted on p. 35 are more or less correct. Hence, if I learn the fact about Faraday, I come to know it, and *a fortiori* to believe it.

At least two strands of belief theory heavily emphasise language: (1) traditional 'propositional' views of belief, according to which, when Jones believes that *p*, he has an attitude to a proposition; (2) more recent theories such as that of Jerry Fodor, according to which to have a belief is to be related in a certain way to a mental representation. If Jones believes that he would be lighter on the moon than he is on Earth, then he has a relationship to a mental representation which means that (expresses the proposition that) Jones would be lighter on the moon than he is on Earth (Fodor, 1991, p. 35).

On the basis of either (1) or (2), we discover whether Jones believes that Faraday discovered the dynamo from whether Jones utters sentences to state the Faraday fact in suitable ways and in suitable contexts. It seems to be satisfactory to report such beliefs in words, which may include mathematical expressions if necessary. For instance: Jones believes that his neighbour has stolen his car; Einstein believes that $E = MC^2$.

Traditional propositional belief theory, and the views of Fodor, are likely to be 'realist' in character. They will assume that something specific about a believer 'makes it true' that they have a particular belief. What is supposed to 'make it true' that Jones believes that p? One way of expressing a realist response is to assert that it is true just when Jones is in a certain kind of state. Before Jones believed that p, he was not in this state, and if he lost the belief that p, he would no longer be in this state. If Jones believes that p, and Brown believes that p, then according to this way of thinking their beliefs have the same content. However much they may differ from each other in other ways, they will, according to this perspective at least, resemble each other in both being in a certain kind of state.

This is one way, then, of characterising a form of *realism* about belief ascriptions. To help us consider whether such realism is appropriate, it is useful at this point to note a simple example where realism in the above sense is uncontroversial: 'The block is cubical' is true, if it is true, in virtue of the block being in such and such a type of state, i.e. a state of being cubical. It is also in virtue of this state that 'The block is not cubical' is false.

A corresponding realism for 'Jones believes that p' would run as follows. If it is true, it is true in virtue of Jones being in a state of a certain type, and it is also in virtue of this state that 'Jones does not believe that p' is false. At a given time, if we ask whether or not Jones believes that p, an affirmative or a negative answer may be objectively correct. If the affirmative answer is correct, this excludes the correctness of the negative answer, and vice versa.

Many objections to this realism are familiar from the literature and have a broadly Wittgensteinian pedigree. Should any attributions purporting to say something about someone's mental or psychological situation be regarded as 'realist'? I think so, and examples are useful to contrast with the appropriate account eventually to be given for belief and other propositional attitudes.

Some of our psychological motivation for realism about belief ascriptions rests on the thought that they resemble pain ascriptions, or ascriptions of other mental states of which we are 'directly aware'. Now realism for pain ascriptions is surely correct. 'Jones is in pain' is true because Jones is in a particular kind of state which is persisting; in virtue of that same state 'Jones is not in pain' is false. We feel very confident of the realist character of pain ascriptions, since we know 'directly' when we are in pain. We can almost, so to speak, literally feel the impossibility of the joint truth of 'I am in pain' and 'I am not in pain'.

The 'directness' of our access has proved notoriously difficult to characterise. I am content here to speak of 'mediate' and 'immediate' objects of awareness. Conscious mental states such as being in pain fall of course into the 'immediate' category. I follow Frank Jackson (1977) in making the immediate/mediate distinction thus. A mediate object of perception for a person S at time *t* occurs if S sees *x* at *t*, and there is a *y* such that *x* is not *y*, and S sees *x* in virtue of seeing *y*. Jackson explains that an immediate object of perception is one that is not mediate. I shall assume that it is legitimate to generalise from Jackson's 'perception' to a more unspecific 'awareness'. Pain on this definition will be an immediate object of awareness. I do not become aware of my pain in virtue of being aware of something else.

A crude belief realism might well incorporate the following claim: having an attitude towards a proposition, this characterised as some kind of state of the individual believer to which he has introspective access and for the existence of which he is the best authority, resembles being in pain. So when Jones believes that *p*, he can be directly aware of the situation that makes 'Jones believes that *p*' true.

One obvious difference between pain and belief is that I cannot be *immediately* aware that I believe that *p*. I can, of course, be immediately aware of a conscious feeling of conviction that *p*. But my belief that *p* cannot be identified with such a feeling of conviction, and hence though I can of course on occasion become aware that I believe that *p* in virtue of being aware of feelings of conviction, this awareness will not be an immediate awareness.

If believing that *p* were identical with having a conscious feeling of assent to *p*, then whilst asleep or unconscious I would no longer believe that *p*. This is a traditional and standard point. But, whilst it would be peculiar to observe of Jones that he is asleep yet still believes that $2+2=4$, the peculiarity arises from the fact that we cannot think of a sensible context for such a remark. It is still true for all that. Further, if believing that *p* were identical with having a conscious feeling of assent that *p*, then it would be impossible for me to have that feeling of assent without believing that *p*. But this is not impossible, as the following example shows.

Suppose that I feel convinced that I believe that on average over a spread of several years the black children in my class have the same range of intelligence as the white children. I may not think about this very much, but when I do, or if I am asked, I have a strong feeling of assent to the statement that they have the same range of intelligence. Research is carried out on my classroom performance over a period of time, and it is found that I consistently provide easier work in English and maths for black children than for 'otherwise comparable' white children.

The suggestion is made that I actually do not believe that on average black children have the same range of intelligence as the white children. My attitude is said to manifest a kind of racism. Now I could protest in all kinds of ways at this accusation; I could raise cogent questions about the quality of the research, and how it was established that pupils were 'otherwise comparable'. All that is required, however from this example is the *possibility in principle* that those accusing me of a form of racism are correct. It seems clear that this possibility exists. I might not have possessed the belief which, when I consciously entertained it, I thought that I did possess.

It follows from this that I cannot have immediate awareness of my belief that *p*. Nonetheless, it is obvious that I often have mediate awareness of my belief that *p*, and achieve this in virtue of my immediate awareness of my feeling that I believe that *p*. The example above is unusual, and in the vast majority of cases when I think I believe that *p* then I do. Nevertheless, the fact that I cannot have immediate awareness of my belief that *p* cuts away some of the ground for asserting parallels between pain ascriptions and belief ascriptions. Now if belief states are not conscious states, what are they supposed to be?

We discover what someone believes from their speech and behaviour. We discover what we believe frequently from our own conscious feelings of conviction, and perhaps in a few cases also by noting in a detached fashion patterns of our own behaviour. The managing director believes he is not prejudiced against female applicants for vacancies, but when he looks back at a series of appointments he has made over the last ten years, and re-examines the merits of the various candidates, he decides that he must have various negative beliefs about women. Before he conducts this review of his conduct, he is under the impression that he lacks such negative beliefs.

So belief is in some way linked to behaviour, and to a range of conscious states, even though it cannot be identified with these items. Dispositional theories of belief have a long history. My having a belief might be thought to involve dispositions to behave and to feel in certain ways in given circumstances. A 'realist' view of dispositions highlights an underlying persistent structure which explains behaviour. The persistent structure provides something in virtue of which the claim that the disposition is possessed even if never exercised can be granted a truth value.

I want to follow up this alleged parallel between the dispositions of substances, such as the solubility of salt, and dispositions with which beliefs might be thought to be identified. The ways in which the supposed correspondences break down are quite illuminating. When this is understood, several steps will have been taken in the direction of the justification of a loose functional account of belief, with its important implications for the limits of educational assessment.

Salt is disposed to behave in such and such ways when placed in appropriate solvents; even if it is never dissolved, we are prepared to assert the truth of counter-factual conditionals to the effect that it would have done such and such if it had been immersed. A 'realist' disposition is thought of as having an underlying state which explains its behaviour in certain situations, and our knowledge of the possession of which justifies our counter-factual claims. This underlying state in the case of salt would concern aspects of its atomic and chemical properties.

On this account, one and the same type of underlying structure could explain the possession of several distinct dispositions. For instance, a salt crystal has a particular molecular structure. This may ground both its solubility in water, and its fragility (Prior, 1985). Accordingly, a so-called 'type-type identity' between dispositions and the intrinsic states of the objects which ground them must be rejected. Further, the same (type) disposition might be grounded in different ways in different substances. For instance, the power to produce a certain electro-motive force may derive from a device's having a certain chemical constitution, like an electrolytic cell, or from a device's having a certain physical constitution, like an electro-magnetic generator (Harré, 1978).

But the persistence of the 'ground' of the disposition, and its re-identifiability over time, provides an essential background to our practices of identifying and re-identifying the disposition itself. Ryle (1949) is responsible for the familiar distinction between single-track and multi-track dispositions. The idea is that some dispositions involve specific kinds of events, whereas others are implicated in a whole range. Solubility-in-water is a reasonable candidate for single trackhood. There is some scope for variation in speed, and whether the resulting solution is coloured, but that is about it. Being magnetic in contrast might show itself through attracting or repelling other objects, inducing current in a coil, causing iron filings to display themselves in characteristic patterns, and so on. It is evident that there is no absolute distinction between single-track and multi-track. It depends how dispositions are identified and counted. For instance, should we count fragility as the disposition to break into any number of pieces given such and such an impact in such and such circumstances? Or ought we to say that *one* disposition results in breaking into twelve pieces or less, while *another* gives more than twelve pieces? Our classifications here will reflect practical interests, rather than any scientifically grounded divisions.

Granting a certain arbitrariness to the question of whether a disposition is multi-track or otherwise, the issue of the explanation of its presence by underlying atomic structures and the like is especially important in cases which are very obviously multi-track. Something is required to support the practice of identifying the iron repelling another magnet as exhibiting the *same disposition* as it did when it induced the current in the coil. The glue that so to speak binds together attracting and repelling iron objects, inducing electric currents in certain circumstances, encouraging iron filings to fall into characteristic patterns, etc., is the underlying arrangement of atoms and electrons which serves to explain this range of phenomena.

Where very different substances exhibited similar dispositions we might look to similarities in underlying structures. For instance, if X and Y are both soluble in water, we might anticipate at least the possibility that they resemble each other in some crucial respect. However, we would be open to the possibility that there was nothing common to them both: that the explanation of X's solubility referred to a very different kind of underlying structure from the explanation of Y's solubility. *There are insuperable difficulties in transferring this model to belief*

In the case of straightforward single-track dispositions such as fragility, we appear to be able to identify and re-identify the disposition through observation of the substance behaving 'in the same kind of way' today as it did yesterday. Yesterday I hit the stone with my geological hammer, and it broke into several pieces. Today I hit one of the pieces with a similar blow, and it fragments into several more. Whatever the stone is made of was brittle yesterday, and is still brittle today. I have no idea what it is about the molecular structure of the material making up the stone which explains its brittleness. While my ignorance in the case of 'being magnetic' is equally complete, we have seen that the explanatory underlying structure plays a crucial role in enabling judgements that it is the 'same disposition again' to be made.

If belief involves, or may be identified with, dispositional properties, these will be par excellence multi-track. Given appropriate assumptions about other beliefs, wants and intentions on the part of the believer, virtually any behaviour whatever can manifest a particular belief. As Armstrong appreciated, without going on to draw the 'anti-realist' view of belief which I would defend, 'the characteristic manifestations of a belief can only be identified as manifestations of the belief by reference back to the belief' (Armstrong, 1973, p. 17). To believe that *p* is not to be disposed to behave in any specific way in a specific circumstance. Hence something corresponding to the glue that holds together the multifaceted disposition of being magnetic needs to be available for belief.

A search for such glue will prove unsuccessful. First, nothing corresponds in the mind or brain to the underlying atomic and chemical properties which are responsible for the dispositions of salt. If we subscribe to some kind of materialist mind–brain identity theory, the most plausible version around I take to be Davidson's 'Anomalous Monism' (Davidson, 1970). According to this theory, individual mental events are identical to individual brain events, but types of mental or psychological events are not identical to types of neurophysiological events. If I believe today that Michael Faraday invented the dynamo, then the specific event of my believing this is identical with particular goings-on in my brain today. If Jones shares my belief, his specific psychological event (or persisting state) is identical with a neurophysiological going-on in his brain today. It is an empirical question whether there would be anything in common between his brain and mine in virtue of our shared belief. Current knowledge of the brain does not point in this direction. Anomalous monism would not even give us a common factor between Jones believing that p at t, and Jones believing that p at t + 1. Neurophysiology does not suggest that a brain state of a similar type is necessary at t + 1 for Jones to have the same belief as the one he held at t.[1]

A dualist rejecting token-token identity theories can do no better. We have seen that beliefs cannot be identified with conscious states. There is no underlying mental 'substratum' with which the base of dispositions can plausibly be identified. The contrast with pain ascriptions illuminates the point. If we are 'token-token' identity theorists, we will probably concede that the brain event which is Jones having a pain at a given time might well differ from the event purportedly identifiable with Smith having a pain. Or Jones having a pain tomorrow may involve a very different brain event from the one identified with his having a pain today. Nevertheless, pains all share obvious 'felt' qualities. There is nothing corresponding to this for belief. Even if I did have a particular conscious experience throughout the time I believed that p, this experience could not be identified with my having the belief.

In view of arguments of these kinds many philosophers have opted for what is sometimes known as a 'functional' account of belief. As I sketched earlier in the section on belief holism, such an account suggests that attributing beliefs is part of an explanation of someone's behaviour. To understand the nature of this functionalism rather better, we are invited to compare being water with being an airfoil (Fodor and Lepore, 1992, p. 115). What accounts for the various properties and dispositions of water, and indeed what makes water to be water, is that its underlying structure is H_2O. On the other hand, an airfoil can be defined in terms of the way it behaves when passing through a liquid or gaseous environment, and the way it relates to these environments. The specific microstructure of airfoils is not really significant. Beliefs are thought to be more like airfoils than like water. Their properties are defined in terms of their interactions with other beliefs and with other aspects of rational agents such as desires and intentions. If there were such a thing as the underlying structure of a belief, and I have argued that there could not be, it would play no part in determining the properties of the belief. Even the language of the observations in this paragraph is still misleading, since it still may appear that individual beliefs are being referred to.

To sum up the conclusions of this chapter, I have argued that a realist account in virtue of which a *de dicto* belief report is true or false should be abandoned. Beliefs should not be seen as discretely identifiable entities. In the face of someone's behaviour and speech we have to perform complex acts of interpretation, in which we impute intentions and beliefs to the person concerned and characterise actions. If we ask whether someone has a particular belief at a particular time, the answer given cannot be said to be true or false in any absolute sense. Their assigned beliefs, intentions and actions are interdependent. If we change one element the others must change too.

This is not to suggest that any one interpretation is as good as any other. Evidently some interpretations are more 'appropriate' than others. Criteria for appropriateness are shared by the adult community who have a basic consensus on principles for interpreting the behaviour and speech of others which take account of their context, both physical and cultural.

These observations about interpretation do not only apply to situations in which we are making judgements about the beliefs, intentions and actions of others. When I make judgements about what I myself believe, my position in logic is similar. I may have immediate awareness of feelings of conviction, consciousness of intentions, and so forth. In virtue of these, and of my knowledge of my patterns of action, I reach a verdict about what I believe. This will only sometimes be a conscious process. There is nothing about me in virtue of which a specific verdict is objectively correct.

Interpretations of beliefs, intentions and actions are in a sense judgements which refer loosely to a person's cognitive state and agency in the widest sense. Having taken the philosophical discussion this far, it is now appropriate to consider the implications of the results for educational assessment.

NOTES

1. The truth of anomalous monism is not unquestioned. 'The uniformity of structure and function of the human brain supports an identity between types of (human) psychological

states and types of (human) physiological states . . . researchers have found uniform physical abnormalities underlying abnormal psychological states — for example, people with obsessions and compulsions . . . have uniform underlying physical abnormalities'. Reznek, L. (1991), *The Philosophical Defence of Psychiatry* (London, Routledge), p. 149. Some broad-brush structural features might correlate with types of psychological state. But the brain is extremely complex, and the idea that there might be fine-grained brain correspondences to go with correspondences in belief is not supported by available evidence.

Chapter 5
Implications for Assessment

We have now completed some important groundwork, to which we will need to refer when mounting a critique of educational assessment. Some time has been spent on the kind of literacy and numeracy in which the state is likely to interest itself. Key elements turned out to be the usability and applicability of the knowledge and skills in question, and the requirement that a significant proportion of the knowledge was 'proper' or 'rich', namely knowledge which was at least to a degree understood. It became clear that the understood knowledge involved in literacy and numeracy should involve little or no deference to the expertise of others, and that understanding is closely bound up with the extent to which the beliefs and concepts concerned are appropriately 'connected'. Beliefs, on a holist perspective, figure in belief reports as the results of a complex process of interpretation, and cannot be identified as discrete items in themselves. Any thought that it is possible to identify quite precisely that someone has a particular belief with an identifiable specific content does not square with the dispositional/functional account of belief developed in the last chapter.

An important thread running through the discussion was the availability of a range of styles in which someone's knowledge or belief can be reported upon. Some of these styles of reporting may attend closely to what is thought to be in the knower's mind. Others in contrast explicitly incorporate references to the real world independently of the knower, at least as the real world is believed to be by the person reporting the belief.

We now begin to discuss the implications for various kinds of educational assessment. It will be argued that there are principled limitations to any attempts to assess rich knowledge and skills. In this chapter, it is assumed that there are no theoretical objections to the conception of rich knowledge and skills *per se*, and the associated possession of adequate cognitive maps. My claim for the time being will be that if there *could* be such an achievement as 'proper' knowledge then there is in principle no form of educational assessment which could detect its presence with any kind of accuracy or precision.

This will be an interim position only. I proceed to argue in Chapter 6 that conceptions of rich knowledge resist precise conceptualisation of a kind which would be required for assessment to be used to hold schools to account, and to support efforts to improve the match of teaching and task to pupil attainment. Moreover several of the limitations inherent in educational assessment addressed first in this chapter will be pursued in more depth in later discussion.

It follows from the loose dispositional account of belief defended in the last chapter that, in the final analysis, aspirations to 'discover' in detail the contents of a pupil's mind are based on an illusion. The illusion is that behind behaviour are minds populated by specific and identifiable beliefs, giving rise to the idea that if only we could probe effectively enough we could find out what is there. The reality is a more complex and elusive situation, in which interpretations are made of the mind-states of others. These interpretations require many assumptions which it would be difficult to make wholly explicit. A full appreciation of a loose dispositional/functional account of belief undermines much contemporary assessment practice in education. To some extent I am compelled to set this radically sceptical position on one side in some of the following discussion. However the principled limitations on our capacities to detect whether others possess specific knowledge items will be taken up once more when we come to discuss ideas about matching in Chapter 7.

WRITTEN ASSESSMENT

Suppose we want to find out what the pupil knows about Michael Faraday. An appropriately worded written test may prompt her to write some sentences about Faraday which are relevant to the questions set. In the light of our discussion of holism we can appreciate that Faraday propositions are connected to a huge variety of others. We also understand that we cannot attribute Faraday *beliefs* to our pupil unless we assume her possession of an indefinite number of other beliefs with an appropriate content. If we are claiming to discern that she has Faraday beliefs with a measure of understanding, and for which she can offer some justification without undue deference to 'experts', we are assuming again that she holds other beliefs. We are judging in addition that these are appropriately connected to her Faraday *beliefs*, and that she correctly identifies the nature of at least some of these connections.

Defenders of written tests can of course argue that the quality of this more extended knowledge can also be tapped within a written examination. Examiners can come to understand as well as anyone else the ways in which various areas of knowledge are or should be connected. Such insights can guide the framing of examination questions. However I would contend that, in the light of the depth and richness of background content germane to Faraday knowledge, the most skilfully devised written test is inevitably severely limited in principle.

Further, the pupil would and should be able to manifest the relevant knowledge and understanding in a whole range of *practical* contexts. The point could be argued to hold good in a wealth of scientific and mathematical examples, especially with younger pupils. It could not be defended so convincingly in connection with the mastery of more abstract subject matter, especially in cases of assessing older pupils and adults.

Consider several pupils who have some knowledge and under- standing of Faraday. Individuals will have made widely varying ranges of connections between their collections of Faraday concepts. (And such sets of concepts may be substantial.) Some may well hold connections to obtain which in fact do not. Moreover, they may have formed links to false beliefs or confused concepts. Others will have made very few connections, and may have done little more than memorise material about Faraday from a book. They may only be able to parrot this information, given an appropriate stimulus. Perhaps, if their language skills are a little more sophisticated, they can regurgitate the content on demand in different terminology. *Correct written responses will not distinguish between the range of candidates as described.*

It might be thought that examiners could be sufficiently ingenious to encourage candidates to display the quality of their own cognitive maps, and that perhaps examiners already do. Questions could be devised to provoke candidates in effect to articulate a range of the connections they have framed between specific content with which the examiners are concerned and other relevant concepts and beliefs. This suggestion may seem attractive for a moment, until we start trying to imagine what kinds of tasks would achieve the desired object. Some of the connections made by the candidate between the specific content of interest to the examiners and other concepts and beliefs will be 'significant' (and correct or appropriate in some way) while other connections will not. To enable consistent marking, examiners might well have to try to create a model of a network of connections which they would deem appropriate. Markers would employ this model to check candidates' answers. Candidates' cognitive maps would in some sense need to correspond to the 'official' map promulgated by the examiners.

There are severe practical problems about this proposal. It would be very difficult to judge how extensive a network should be expected. Examiners and examinees have limited time at their disposal. It would be quite impossible to check how well candidates understood items on the 'periphery' of their maps. Such items could enjoy healthy existence in virtue of links to other material, some of which would not be and could never be within the scope of the official network. This material together with its links would inevitably evade the scrutiny of the examiners.

More fundamental objections also may be raised. The official map would need to become part of the syllabus. While we should not exaggerate the degree to which candidates' idiosyncratic knowledge bases will vary one from another at the beginning of the course to be examined, there will inevitably be variation. The official map cannot take account of this. In consequence if a candidate 'learns up' the official map this may well have to be acquired in a fashion which leaves it disconnected, so to speak, from the rest of his knowledge base. Linking the official map with the rest of his knowledge may not seem relevant to the aim of producing the official set of connected ideas on demand.

Now it would of course be perfectly possible for a candidate to refuse to go down this path. A strong candidate with the help of a teacher with integrity might seek to avoid such a narrow-minded attitude to the test. Instead, much time and energy might be spent ensuring that the official content and its associated 'map' was suitably embedded in and tied to a candidate's personal knowledge base. Yet the damaging accusation against written assessment retains its force. The assessment fails to distinguish between candidates who have simply sought to 'crack the system' and those who have engaged in a search for 'real knowledge', hoping that the fruits of their labours will still manifest themselves in terms of good scores.

Reliable written tests are tests which give consistent results. To achieve this reliability, they need to be highly specific. No ambiguity in marking criteria can be tolerated. The tests will need to be 'closed'. That is to say, tasks must not be set which admit of a range of solutions. One correct response only, carefully detailed by the examiners, should be countenanced. Those devising written tests may be very conscious of this limitation, and strive to overcome it by building in more challenging and thought-provoking test items prompting more flexible responses by the candidates.

Yet in the end the examiners have to be entirely precise about what in the examination is to count as knowing X about Faraday. This constraint, to be effective, must detach knowing X from the rest of each pupil's idiosyncratic network of concepts and beliefs. A given response is demanded from the pupil, regardless of how the 'knowledge' of which this response is supposed to be the expression is connected up to other content known by the pupil. In consequence at least for examination purposes it makes knowing X into something 'thin': something which of itself is not manifestable in a variety of practical contexts or is not usable and applicable. This is not the kind of knowledge in which a flourishing industrial economy has any stake. (We will need to say much more about the ideas of reliability and validity in Chapter 8, and to elaborate further the argument about disconnected pupil performances when we consider the challenge of providing a common language in which to report pupil achievement.)

Written assessment has severe limitations. Many of its difficulties are well-known. The arguments presented above are, I suspect, restatements of what many education professionals have been thinking for decades. Yet there is little sign of a radical move away from written assessment, despite flirtations with 'authentic' assessment, practical tests and the like.

I believe that one of the reasons this extraordinary state of affairs continues for so long is that we do not distinguish sufficiently keenly between the different ways in which a pupil's set of beliefs or their knowledge may be reported on. When an appropriate written response is forthcoming in a test we may characterise the response as a manifestation of given knowledge. However, our narrative about the given knowledge is very likely to incorporate some of our own beliefs about the real world and the characteristics of key concepts involved. Typically we will fail to be sufficiently modest in our attempt to capture 'what is in the pupil's mind'. We project our adult sets of concepts onto the minds of pupils, and proceed to slide into speaking of their personal grasp of these concepts. This confusion helps to mask the fundamental inadequacy of much written assessment.

MAKING JUDGEMENTS ABOUT RICH COGNITIVE ACHIEVEMENT ON THE BASIS OF LIMITED SAMPLES OF BEHAVIOUR

In the account of belief offered in the last chapter it became clear that language, whether written or spoken, is only part of the behaviour we use when attributing beliefs or knowledge to others. We need now to consider how far non-verbal behaviour can supplement evidence in the form of pupil language in order to aid educational assessment.

Some years ago when writing about a related topic (Davis, 1986) I suggested that in science contexts pupils' capacities to produce verbal or symbolic formulations could prove extremely misleading if taken alone as the basis of an assessment of their scientific knowledge. A secondary pupil might have a verbal or symbolic mastery of Newtonian mechanics. She says appropriate things such as that *force* is *mass × acceleration*, that *acceleration* is increase of *velocity* over time, that *bodies not acted upon by forces* continue with the same *velocity* in a *straight line*, and so forth. She may also be able to solve problems in examination papers in which masses have to be calculated given certain other information.

However, that same pupil when involved in a school engineering project to construct a model of a bridge, or create an electric powered car, may make all kinds of decisions which are not consistent with the fact that Newtonian mechanics approximately applies to the devices she is helping to create. Now it would be perfectly possible to explain her failures in terms of a lack of practical skills of various kinds. Alternatively, it might be thought that she had incorrect beliefs about the nature of some of the materials being used. If there were ways of obtaining further evidence about these possibilities, through talking to her or observing how she behaved in yet other circumstances, we might conclude that she did not lack relevant practical skills, and that she did not have idiosyncratic beliefs about the materials. One of the remaining hypotheses about her case might be this. She has failed to associate her abstract understanding of the concepts involved in Newtonian mechanics with the behaviour of real objects which the science is designed to explain. This would be a very significant kind of limitation in her scientific understanding.

It may also be claimed, though it is not clear how independent this new claim would be from the one just cited, that she is unable to 'use and apply' her knowledge about Newtonian mechanics, in one or more of the senses of 'use and apply' which we canvassed in Chapter 2.

Assessment restricted to written or verbal forms could not detect limitations of this type. We can also see that it would not help even if the written or oral assessment was supplemented with some practical tests. For it would be perfectly possible for the girl to learn how to perform well on these specific tests and still not make the 'connections' required for 'proper knowledge' of Newtonian mechanics.

Much of the argument here has concentrated on the example of written performance, since this is still the dominant paradigm in contemporary educational assessment. Furthermore, verbal performance appeared to offer a particularly obvious pointer to the content of the mind behind the performance. Note however that the general argument is equally relevant to the inherent restrictions of *any limited set of performances* being used as the basis on which judgements are made about the nature of and extent of pupils' rich knowledge.

Some may wonder whether there are really no elements within literacy and numeracy, or indeed in other subject areas, which could appropriately and accurately be assessed by means of written tests or relatively circumscribed performances. Any search for answers should be guided by our reflections on holism and the nature of belief itself.

Written assessment may be quite good at tapping the extent to which candidates have assimilated factual material in a superficial fashion. It should be conceded that we cannot rule out altogether the possibility that such assimilated material may prove useful to the candidate or to others. However, it is notorious that material learned in this fashion is forgotten by the majority of learners in a very short time.

'Know-how' which is relatively unsaturated with declarative knowledge also appears to be susceptible to assessment through strictly limited sampling of behaviour. For it is declarative knowledge involving beliefs connected in clusters which resists assessment of this kind.

I do not intend to discuss candidates for 'knowledge unsaturatedness' in any depth, but the 'ability' to write by hand to a reasonable standard, to recognise specific words in print and pronounce them correctly, and to provide correct answers when asked to add mentally a pair of two-digit numbers, seem plausible examples. Possibly Associated Board Music exams probe 'skills' of a similar order, including the 'ability' to clap back the rhythm of a short melody after it has been played twice by the examiner, and to identify correctly the middle note of a three-note chord played on the piano. We might also consider the fact that in a driving test the examiner asks the candidate to perform an emergency stop. Such a limited practical test seems a reasonable way of probing whether the candidate can in fact do what is required.

There is likely to be argument over the extent to which particular areas of knowledge or competence may be analysed into 'thin' know-how of this kind. The debate will probably parallel disputes more than two decades ago about whether the taxonomies of behavioural objectives really succeeded in capturing the nature of the knowledge they purported to represent (Bloom, 1956; Stenhouse, 1975). To continue the 'connection' metaphor, imagine that a substantial proportion of literacy and numeracy could apparently be analysed into thin know-how. (I do not in fact think that this is possible.) There would still be something left out. The possessor of these putative discrete competencies would need to understand something of the relationships between their possible functions to be able to make use of them in an intelligent way. In fact, this point is probably just another way of arguing that literacy and numeracy cannot be analysed in this fashion.

Winch and Gingell (1996) objected to ancestors of this argument on the grounds that understanding and the richness of knowledge is a matter of degree. The emphasis on holistic accounts of knowledge and belief, they asserted, confused the end point of education with the stages through which pupils might need to pass. The extent and comprehensiveness of the connections obtaining between a given knowledge item possessed by a ten year-old, say that plants need water to grow, and the rest of their knowledge will differ appreciably from that of the eighteen year-old in respect of the same biological fact. There is nothing whatever wrong with this, they urged, and indeed how could it be otherwise? Winch and Gingell felt that my criticism of assessment somehow assumed that the ten year-old should be in the position of the eighteen year-old.

My response is to accept the difference between the ten year-old and the eighteen year-old, but to urge that the holistic features of belief and of concepts obtain regardless of the degree of richness concerned. It is true that children must begin somewhere, but by the time they reach school age their networks are already complex if in some ways immature. The expectations by teachers or examiners should in some broad sense be appropriate to the age of the pupils being assessed, but this does not seem to me to detract from the force of the critique of assessment offered here.

CONCLUSION

Winch and Gingell (1996) reacted to a more modest version of the above critique of assessment with incredulity. Their concern was that it exemplified a destructive scepticism about whether anyone has learned anything. The scepticism is unwarranted, they argue, since it assumes that knowledge items and abilities are only available in the kinds of contexts in which they were learned. They assert that 'there is no good reason to think that practical contexts are sufficiently different from assessment situations so that knowledge will not be properly measured'.

I do not in fact embrace any kind of global scepticism about the possibility of discovering whether someone has learned, but am certainly mounting arguments implying serious caution in a carefully detailed series of cases. My special concern is the limited capacity of educational assessment to probe rich knowledge.

Now it is often a good ploy to exaggerate the conclusions of one's opponent and then to dismiss them as obviously absurd, and I suspect that this may be going on here. I am well aware that part of what it is to be human is to be able to arrive at reasonable conclusions about what others are thinking, feeling and knowing. I certainly do not seek to deny this. I am claiming that educational assessment in some guises attempts to wrench this basic aspect of humanity in the direction of a spurious scientific rigour.

I agree, however, that the issue of whether knowledge or abilities 'transfer' is a crucial one in my assault on educational assessment. My criticisms of written forms of assessment, and of any limited sampling of pupil behaviour whether verbal or otherwise in order to make judgements about their cognitive achievements, have been concerned about the potential 'isolation' of the test responses from the rest of their knowledge. By implication, this is a concern about the way their test behaviour may be insulated from the kind of behaviour they would produce in contexts other than the examination room or test context. Can the Associated Board candidate who claps back a rhythm played to her also mimic rhythms suggested by the conductor of the orchestra in which she is playing? Does the pupil who can insert capital letters and full stops appropriately into unpunctuated prose succeed in using capitals and full stops properly in her own free writing?

This seems to be yet another way of describing the problem about transfer. Accordingly I now turn to discuss this at some length.

Chapter 6
Transfer, Abilities and Rules

The issue of 'transfer' appears to be conceptually related to several standard philosophical topics. These are the problem of induction, the nature of powers and dispositions, vagueness and metaphor, and the rule-following considerations deriving from Wittgenstein and from both his exponents and detractors. In this chapter I offer an extensive discussion in which I in turn compare and contrast 'transfer' with these topics, in an effort to make clear what the transfer 'problem' is, and what it is not. I will be arguing that transfer resists precise characterisation of the kind required for accountability through assessment.

A teacher can only introduce knowledge or skill in a limited range of situations. The idea is that pupils 'generalise', and use and apply their knowledge in an indefinite variety of new circumstances. Presumably without a belief in transfer our modern industrial economy would place little faith in school achievements. Excitement about assessment results is only well founded if (a) pupil knowledge and understanding 'transfers' to performance in assessment contexts, (b) the latter 'transfers' to useful performance in employment, and (c) 'transfer' is a transitive relation, so that (a) and (b) entail that pupil knowledge and understanding transfer to useful performance in employment.

It has often been pointed out that without transfer no learning would take place. Indeed, a classic authority (Thorndike, 1914) denied the distinction between learning and transfer. Contemporary psychologists (e.g. Butterfield, Slocum and Nelson, 1993) would see the interesting research questions focusing on the fact that some teaching produces reliably improved performance across a broader range of circumstances than other teaching. They see no 'principled difference between learning and transfer' (p. 194).

Oddly enough, faith in transfer used to be more overt (and less plausible). Training in the classics was supposed to fit students for the British Civil Service. Several years' study of Ancient Greek would make civil servants better able to meet the demands of their workplace than they would otherwise have been. The doctrine of 'formal discipline', owing something perhaps to Aristotle's faculty view of the mind, was classically attacked by the psychologist Thorndike, who concluded that transfer was only possible between one kind of activity and another where there were identical elements (Singley and Anderson, 1989).

Modern school curricula purport to offer activities and contexts 'closer' to the activities in which the pupils will engage as adult employees. Children take part in 'work experience', for example. Presumably part of the rationale for this is that they are supposed to gain some grasp of the kinds of contexts in which they are likely to have to use and apply their school knowledge.

PSYCHOMETRICS, TRAIT DISCOURSE AND TRANSFER

A significant element in the history of psychometrics has been the search for tests whose results 'transfer', which predict performance in a whole wealth of contexts. The classic example was of course the IQ test. Needless to say, attempts to assess 'intelligence' could not help the state make education more accountable unless intelligence could actually be 'developed' by schools. Traditionally intelligence has been conceptualised as a trait which cannot be acquired in the short term as a result of teaching. This view would be held even by those acknowledging the substantial role of environmental influences on the development of intelligence.

In recent years fresh claims have been made that generic capacities, 'thinking skills' for instance, can be taught, and that these transfer widely to activities in other domains and subjects (e.g. Adey, P., Shayer, M. and Yates, C., 1989). These alleged general capacities seem to be related to certain conceptions of intelligence.

Within the psychometric tradition, 'valid' tests are said be those that measure what they are supposed to measure. 'Measuring' through predictions of various kinds has figured centrally in some conceptions of validity. The predictions might be of success levels in other kinds of examinations or tests, or in jobs. These measured phenomena are open to public observation.

Another influential line of thought about validity is that a test has 'construct validity' if it measures some kind of underlying (and unseen) trait, ability or competence, referred to as a 'construct'. One classic construct was the so-called 'general ability' of intelligence. More is said about validity in Chapter 8.

It would be a mistake to think that the idea of a 'construct' should be restricted to psychometrics discourse. In effect all assessment assumes the possibility and coherence of a whole range of constructs, from the highly specific to the very general. Sometimes a false contrast is drawn between what can be measured 'directly' and what can be measured 'indirectly'. For instance, Bartram (1990) asserts that 'Many tests are designed to measure traits that are hypothetical' (p. 77). This suggests that other traits might be 'actual'. How exactly is that supposed to be possible? Even if we say that Jones can throw the ball, thereby crediting him with something overtly physical and 'directly' observable, we still in a sense need to invoke a 'construct' if we are confident about future ball-throwing successes. Even when Jones is not throwing balls, there is something about him which explains the fact that he could throw balls if he chose, and the circumstances were right.

I have explored problems about trait thinking elsewhere (Davis, 1993). Rust and Golombok (1989) refer to 'trait' thinking as part of folk psychology. It serves no explanatory purpose but we are unlikely to be able to eradicate it. They observe:

> There is, of course much argument about the existence or otherwise of 'ability in mathematics' and the nature of such a concept. People do tend to use these concepts . . . How else could an O-level in mathematics, for example, be used by an employer in selecting a person for a job? Certainly it is unlikely that the mathematics syllabus was constructed with any knowledge of this employer's particular job in mind . . . . No, the criteria used in practice . . . involve the use of folk psychological theorizing, and folk psychological constructs by employers . . . . These examinations are seen as measuring folk psychological traits. (p. 33–34).

Arguably some folk-psychological explanations are more reputable than others. If they include personal explanations in terms of wants, intentions and reasons they are here to stay, and could not be replaced by more 'scientific' accounts (Baker, 1995). However I will be contending in this chapter that much 'trait thinking', particularly in educational discourse, should be dispensed with (and there are no obvious scientific replacements on offer).

The next two sections are intended as preliminary explorations of fundamental conceptual issues raised by trait and transfer discourse. My strategy here is to begin to shed light on these areas by considering them in relation first to questions about induction, powers and dispositions, and second to questions about vagueness and fuzzy borders in language use. I believe that one effective route into understanding the nature of the challenges presented by traits and transfer is to compare and contrast them with these two groups of questions.

Suppose we are wondering whether a child will succeed today as she has previously in similar circumstances with the same task. Uncertainty about her performance might have a variety of sources. A theoretical worry based on scepticism about induction is perfectly feasible. Needless to say, the practical man is very unlikely to relate philosophical concerns about induction to any uncertainties he may have about his pupil's performance today. In contrast he will think it relevant to ask whether earlier achievements will transfer to today's performances. Concerns about induction are 'philosophers' problems' whereas transfer questions are very real in education and other contexts.

One of the other reasons for uncertainty about a child's performance today might stem from the involvement of a predicate with 'fuzzy edges'. Where the criteria for using a particular term are less than clear-cut, this may make it difficult to be sure about how the child will act today, if her action incorporates a use of that term. Again, it will prove advantageous to understand how transfer questions are to be distinguished from semantic features of this kind.

INDUCTION, POWERS AND DISPOSITIONS

Suppose a child responds 'eight' on several occasions when asked the question: 'What is eleven minus three?' I may wonder, if momentarily in the grip of Humean scepticism, whether she will be successful tomorrow on a *relevantly similar* problem, or on another example of the *same kind* of problem. When untroubled by philosophical doubt, I simply assume tacitly that induction 'works'. The sun will rise tomorrow because it always has done. Similarly, I feel justified in claiming that tomorrow my pupil will answer 'eight' when I ask her to subtract 3 from 11.

To frame either the optimism about induction, or the Humean scepticism, I rely upon an uncontested conception of similarity and of the possibility that I can judge accurately that a given process, event or state of affairs is *relevantly similar* to a previous instance. There is supposed to be no difficulty about explicating a way in which the sunrises at least in recorded history are similar to each other, and how tomorrow's event will be similar to all the others. Again, when I question my pupil tomorrow about what is left when 3 is taken from 11, it may seem obvious how this question will resemble many previous interrogations. So doubt about her success may seem artificial: mere philosophical posturing. The more general scepticism about induction may be thought to deserve the same charge.

Suppose we change the numbers. Will our pupil answer success-fully if asked tomorrow to subtract 5 from 12? Are we still in a Humean quagmire? Or does our question now amount to a fully-fledged transfer puzzle? We have been asked to imagine that previously the child had no dealings with 'subtractions' other than in the form of questions about 11 and 3. Just one of the difficulties about this thought-experiment is that these engagements with 11 and 3 could scarcely be said to be subtracting. The child would only be 'going through the motions'. It would in fact seem appropriate to characterise her history simply as being trained to say 'eight' when asked a particular question.

We will try again. Imagine that the child has been doing correctly $15-9$, $12-8$, $19-11$, and all the other combinations possible with numbers up to 20. We now might describe her activities more broadly. She has been successful in the past with certain *kinds* of number problems. We will give her another of the *same kind* today ($12-5$), and she will succeed. We might be quite happy to say that all the relevant performances share a common characteristic, namely that of being subtractions. Granting all this, any doubts about today's performance might well be denounced as arcane Humean scepticism. Yet, as before, this interpretation depends crucially on a judgement about resemblance or similarity. It is supposed to be self-evident that $12-5$ is similar in some sense to $19-11$, $15-9$, and so forth. I am not for a moment implying that it is *not* self-evident, but striving to shed a little light on what might be going on here.

In the discussion of belief, we examined the topic of dispositions as possessed by items in the material world. We need to return to this subject, and to compare the above reflections about performances with some elementary thoughts about natural kinds, powers and dispositions.

In the past, when I have hit pieces of gold with a hammer, they have dented quite easily. This rock looks like gold. If I hit it, will it dent? If it is iron pyrites, then it will behave quite differently. If I had known it was definitely gold my question about this piece of rock could well have expressed an induction worry. The latter would run as follows: when in the past gold has been struck in a specified fashion (at room temperature, pressure, etc.) it has always dented. Will my gold be dented when struck in this particular way today?

But as a matter of fact I am uncertain whether the rock is actually a particular element. Does it belongs to a specific *natural kind*? If it does, it will be malleable. Gold is malleable because of its underlying microscopic structure. My uncertainty here need have nothing to do with the classic 'problem' of induction. I could be sure about the behaviour of gold (based on how gold has acted up to now), but not know what to expect from this particular piece of rock.

Returning to the arithmetic, I might wonder how the child would fare with $3-8$. There are various possible reasons for uncertainty here. My doubts could relate to whether this problem is relevantly similar to certain earlier 'subtraction' tasks with other numbers where she did experience success. In particular, I might wonder whether she will be successful because I am not sure whether *she* will see today's problem as another of the same kind as those which she tackled before. Insofar as I am reflecting on similarity questions here, I am not puzzling over the 'problem of induction'. As Singley and Anderson observe (1989, p. 8): 'The question whether there is transfer between tasks often has no dogmatic answer; transfer often depends on whether a common representation of the tasks can be found and communicated to subjects'.

Similarity does not seem to present challenges of the same order in the gold case. True, one denting will never be exactly like another, but in general it seems quite straightforward what is to count as being dented. I can easily recognise whether today's event is relevantly similar to earlier dentings. My own subjective view of whether similarities obtain does not have a significant status in the matter. The similarities obtain, or they do not. My thinking that they obtain remains just that: a personal opinion about the matter which may or may not be objectively correct. Contrast this with my judgement about whether something I am now doing resembles something I did successfully on a past occasion. If, for instance, I do not think of my present action as relevantly similar to something I achieved earlier, this may make the crucial difference to whether I am successful now.

We will need to say much more later about the contrast between the operation of similarity judgements in chemistry, as one instance from science, and similarity judgements made about human performances, contexts in which agents act, and so on.

To sum up this section: both induction and transfer questions involve judgements about the similarity of the current event to previous events. The philosopher who asks about how induction can be justified may take similarity as read, at least to an extent which allows him if he wishes to pursue professional sceptical concerns. The teacher or psychologist on the other hand wondering whether certain previous learning will transfer to today's problem immediately must consider exactly how today's problem resembles and differs from earlier achievements which they see as relevant to today's challenge. *Similarity questions will be central to their investigations.* We can see already that there will be no easy answers to such questions, and neither at least at first sight are there any obvious justifications for any answers which might be forthcoming.

VAGUENESS AND FUZZY BORDERS

Suppose I train a child to say 'blue' when confronted with a range of shades of this colour. Today I have some new curtains, and I wonder whether she will say 'blue'. My doubts may arise because the curtains do not precisely resemble any of her training shades. Specifically, the curtains are a greenish-blue. I am unable to draw a precise boundary to the term 'blue'. I am definite that *these* shades are not blue, that *those* others are blue, but there are some 'between' shades which I cannot classify confidently.

Or we might consider the Wittgensteinian 'Stand in the corner'. The predicate 'in the corner' is at one and the same time perfectly adapted for clear communication, and inherently vague. If I say this to a child, she is likely to know exactly what I mean, and is unlikely to prevaricate with observations such as: 'I don't know where you mean. Is the corner here? Or a few centimetres to the left?'

What counts as 'the corner' does not have clear, well-defined borders. (Wittgenstein makes the point that crediting the predicate with vagueness should not be seen as a criticism. It works perfectly well, and this kind of vagueness 'afflicts' many everyday phrases with which we succeed in communicating information and instructions with admirable clarity.)

Evidently predicates with fuzzy borders may affect my confidence in predicting whether a pupil will achieve on a certain task. It may well be asked whether my hesitation about the child's likely success with $3 - 8$ is of a similar order.

I would want to argue that difficulties about the boundaries of 'blue' seem quite distinct from the problems about the boundaries of 'subtraction'. It simply is not the case that in the example under discussion I am sure that *these* instances are subtractions, that *those* are not, and that there are some problem examples where I am uncertain about whether they are subtractions or not. The issue here is not a matter of fuzzy borderlines. The question whether $3 - 8$ is relevantly similar to $15 - 8$, and thus a case of subtraction, is conceptually both complex and rich. Tightening up linguistic practice, if this were possible, would not address this point at all. It could be argued that characterising $3 - 8$ as 'subtraction' may be seen as a metaphorical extension of the term whose 'literal' uses occur typically in contexts in which the operation may be modelled as physical taking away, or physical comparison to discover the difference. If this is right, it helps us to see how extending 'subtract' differs from, for instance, extending the use of a colour term by adjusting its boundaries. The latter need involve no metaphorical shift of any kind.

Similar comments could be made in relation to the vagueness of phrases such as 'in the corner'. If a pedantic child were to interrogate his teacher about whether his standing three feet from the corner counted as 'standing in the corner', the teacher can respond if she chooses by defining more precisely the use of a phrase which is normally fuzzy at the edges. No move of this kind is going to settle the deeper questions raised by comparing $3 - 8$ to $15 - 8$.

CLASSIFICATION: SUBSTANCES AND THEIR DISPOSITIONAL PROPERTIES; HUMAN PERFORMANCES AND SITUATIONS

Earlier I began to compare the logic of human performance classifications to that of the classification of the powers and dispositions of substances. Let us now continue this line of thought. It will emerge that the differences are more striking than the parallels. I contend that the healthy use of fine-grained trait discourse and associated conceptions of transfer is undermined by the differences which emerge.

Simon Blackburn observes in another connection: 'writers generally agree that there is a distinction between classifications that carve nature at the joints and those that do not, and these kinds, reflecting as they do the particular interests of human beings, surely do not' (Blackburn, 1991, p. 220). I intend to argue that many classifications of human performance, achievement and context involving any kind of knowledge and understanding over and above simple physical skills *could not* 'carve nature at the joints'. This is a stronger thesis than merely that they do not. It requires and will receive a substantial defence.

Part of the case for the differences between cognitive achievements and the powers of substances requires a kind of realism for, say, chemistry, which we cannot defend for discourse about human knowledge, performance and its contexts. A first attempt to state such a scientific realism might run thus: the ways in which items, processes and events are identified and classified in the physical sciences are to a degree independent of our interests and culture.

However, this explanation of realism is insufficient if we wish to contrast it effectively with a view about human activity. For classifications even in the physical sciences must significantly reflect our culture and interests. This might be thought to imply that we would have very different classifications if our culture and society were fundamentally different from the way they are.

I suggest that this point must be conceded, but that a residual scientific realism may still be defended which sets it apart from the status of discourse about human activity. We are still entitled to hold that the ways in which matter behaves quite independently of human beings and their social constructs severely limits the possibility of 'different' chemistries in imaginably different cultures. For instance, the powers and dispositions of gold are importantly different from those of iron regardless of *how we choose to characterise the relevant phenomena and events.* Such realist claims need not commit us to a naive correspondence theory of truth, and, in particular, to any crude account of the way in which scientific propositions might mirror a physical reality existing independently of us.

Here are a few more 'realist' observations about gold: gold over a period of time will behave consistently; its observable dispositions and powers will vary predictably according to its physical context. It may be a solid, a liquid or even a gas. At normal temperatures it is malleable and may be dissolved in aqua regia. Its atomic and molecular structures which typically persist over time may readily be identified and re-identified. These account for its powers and dispositions in a whole range of contexts. *They support the identification and re-identification of its powers and dispositions*, as we saw in Chapter 4.

One fundamental difference between applications of similarity to human performance and to substances has already been noted. With substances, questions arise concerning whether, for instance, this is a sample of the same element, whether this material is exhibiting the same disposition, and so forth, and what 'same' would mean in the answers given. There are two levels of questions about human performances and contexts. At the first level, it can be asked whether a context, situation or performance is similar to or the same as a previous instance, and in what the sameness or similarity consists. At the second level, it can be asked whether an agent *thinks* of a new situation to which she might transfer knowledge or skill as resembling a past situation in which she acquired the knowledge. Or does the agent view a potential action as of the 'same type' as previous actions? In what does sameness or similarity consist at this second level? Further, it is clear that the notion of a 'situation' or 'context' must not be naively construed for instance by assuming that mere physical descriptions, however complex, might suffice. 'Context' includes the actual and perceived cultural environment.

The argument under development in this chapter urges that similarity conceptions often could not in principle support classifications which cut the nature of human activities or contexts 'at the joints'. When one performance is deemed to be relevantly similar to another, then they are likely to be put into a particular category. For instance, several actions may be said to be examples of throwing balls, solving problems or subtractions. This kind of move is essential for transfer questions to be framed. Will *ball throwing* transfer to *flinging javelins*? Will *subtraction* transfer to *giving change in the shop*? Transfer discourse relies logically on a more basic discourse in which questions of similarity and difference have been settled, at least for the time being.

I would argue that the way we categorise pupil performances often reflects our own interests, sets of adult conceptions and cultural context. We assume that it is at least possible for pupils to possess traits answering to our descriptions of their competencies. I think that this is often not the case. Indeed Nelson Goodman contended that the notion of similarity is singularly elusive. It does not in itself, he claims, provide us with a justifiable conceptual framework within which we can count two occurrences repetitions of the same behaviour or experiment (Goodman, 1970). Am I today repeating my behaviour of hitting a tennis ball against a barn door in which I indulged yesterday? For my sequence of movements today is very different. If I experiment twice, have I carried out the same experiment twice? For there will be many differences between the two occasions. Goodman suggested that we make judgements about whether the experiments are sufficiently similar to count as repetitions which depend on our theory. We judge actions to be repetitions depending on our purposes and interests. 'Whether two actions are instances of the same behaviour depends upon how we take them; response to the command, "Do that again," may well be the question: "Do what again? Swat another fly or move choreographically the same way?"' (*ibid.* p. 22).

Adopting aspects of Goodman's perspective, the heart of my argument may be characterised as contrasting: (a) 'theory' which grounds judgements of similarity, and the identification and re-identification of substances and dispositions, for instance in chemistry, and (b) 'theory' within which we ground judgements about the similarity of human activities and contexts.

SITUATED COGNITION THEORY: ITS VIEW OF SIMILARITY

Though they stem from very different intellectual traditions, I see resonances between Goodman's nominalistic observations and writings about so-called 'situated cognition'. For example, Lave and Wenger write: 'Activities, tasks, functions, and understandings do not exist in isolation; they are part of broader systems of relations in which they have meaning. These systems of relations arise out of and are reproduced and developed within social communities, which are in part systems of relations among persons' (1991, p. 53).

If actions and cognitions are 'situated' in this fashion, then similarities between actions, cognitions and so forth presumably do not obtain independently from their social contexts. For agents to see their actions as similar in certain ways to previous performances or their current application of knowledge as making fresh use of the 'same' knowledge, they must learn to construct similarity judgements. They do this in social contexts, in interaction with others.

Contrast the 'situated' character of actions and knowledge with that of substances in chemistry. Well-established theory about substances and their dispositional properties supports judgements, for instance, concerning gold behaving in similar ways in a range of contexts in which it is subjected to blows. These judgements of similarity support the identification and re-identification of properties such as malleability. Judgements made about the similarity of human performances within theories of psychology or of learning would be of a fundamentally different character. This is because the very meaning and identity of many human activities will depend upon the social context in which they are 'situated'. Of course, cases will vary. The 'situatedness' of an action of catching a ball seems so to speak skin-deep. Its meaning and identity turn only superficially on its situation or context. Crucial will be 'objective', straightforwardly observable, non-relational physical features of the event concerned, such as whether the ball after travelling through the air is stopped and retained in someone's hands, and does not fall to the ground. Compare this, for instance, with the 'situatedness' of performances in which pupils 'evaluate their own talk and reflect on how it varies' (DFE, 1995a).

Goodman's conclusions, if true, are necessarily true. His perspective consists of an analytical account of the possible meanings of 'similarity'. By contrast it might be expected that the theses of social theory would be empirical and contingent. I would counter by urging caution lest the logical character of contributions from either philosophy or social theory are stereotyped. Goodman scrutinises possible meanings of the term 'similar'. He points out general features of our social practices associated with similarity judgements which could not be otherwise. In his view there is less about the idea of similarity *per se* than meets the eye: we have to import meaning from our own practices, purposes and theories. At the same time, the detail of particular purposes, practices and theories owned by real people, and how these constrain their similarity judgements, are open to empirical inquiry.

The insights provided by situated cognition theory include analyses of ideas of knowledge, action and context with a logical character very similar to those stemming from action theory and philosophy of mind. Lave *et al.* may not see themselves as analysing the nature of human action, knowledge, understanding and context in principle, but as offering analyses which are open to empirical justification. As a matter of fact, we find in their work a complex and rich hybrid of logical analyses of notions of human action, understanding and meaning, together with empirical (if abstract) suggestions about how actions, understanding and meaning are embedded within particular human practices (e.g. those of midwives, tailors, quartermasters, butchers, alcoholics) and how people learn by participating in these practices.

Some psychologists sympathetic to the ideas of situated learning are also concerned to develop theories of transfer. These are far removed from Thorndike's classic account which relied on a supposedly unproblematic notion of resemblance or 'identity' between activities or situations: 'One mental function or activity improves others insofar as and because they are in part identical with it, because it contains elements common to them' (Thorndike, 1906, p. 246).

Greeno, Moore and Smith (1993) see knowing not as a stable property of an individual, but as a property which is relative to situations. They maintain that it is insufficient to state that cognition is influenced by contexts. They support a more fundamental and radical view to the effect that knowing, reasoning, understanding and so on are relations between cognitive agents and situations 'and it is not meaningful to try to characterise what someone knows apart from situations in which the person engages in cognitive activity' (p. 100). Transfer questions concern how 'learning to participate in an activity in one situation can influence (positively or negatively) one's ability to participate in another activity in a different situation' (*ibid.*). The issue of transfer is 'social'.

Some of these observations seem to me to contain important insights. However, one difficulty about their position is immediately apparent. When they speak of 'one situation' I do not think they mean to refer to a specific datable occasion. I cannot be absolutely certain, since they are not explicit about this. As I understand them, 'one situation' appears rather to refer to 'one *type* of situation'. If my interpretation is correct, they have already helped themselves to notions of similarity which allow them to classify activities in the first place: 'the activities of learning and performance can be defined socially in ways that encourage or discourage efforts to learn in order to transfer to a broader domain of situations, or, in a transfer situation, to try to relate the situation to the person's previous experience' (*ibid.*).

They view the process of situation classification as influenced by social interactions. How agents conceptualize their learning activities and subsequent performances is subject to substantial social definition. So teachers can influence pupils' conceptions of actions and situations in such a way that other situations are seen by pupils as similar, and hence 'transfer' is encouraged. 'The potential for transfer between situations is shaped by the social practices in which the people learn the activities' (*ibid.*, p. 102).

For their purposes, there was no need to discuss the question whether social definitions of performance or situation classifications might or might not correspond to any idea of 'real' or 'natural' kinds to which performances or situations could belong. However, they would be unlikely to find any picture of 'objective' performance or situation classifications coherent, if this picture implied that such classifications could obtain independently of the socially defined conceptualisation imposed by agents. To this extent, their views are consistent with those of Lave and Goodman.

Let us together draw the threads of the argument so far. We learn from Goodman that judgements about sameness and similarity require a 'theory'. In the case of substances, this amounts to the account of their underlying properties which explains their dispositions in a range of contexts. This theory legitimates the identification of dispositional properties such as malleability, and enables us to speak of specific properties persisting over a period of time. We can make statements such as 'The gold is behaving in the same way again' (e.g. being dented when struck). We can predict clearly how gold will behave in the future, taking into account the diverse range of circumstances in which it might be placed. All this is in sharp contrast to the position with respect to human performance and cognition. The very identity and meaning of an action is dependent on its relationship with aspects of its social context. Classification of actions and knowledge reflects human purposes and interests. What counts as 'the same performance again' usually cannot be gleaned from a consideration of the nature of that performance detached from its context and the meaning attached to it by the agent and her community.

ABILITIES, COMPETENCIES, TRAITS AND SKILLS

Conceptions of 'the same performance again' are tied to notions of ability, trait, competence, and so on. I noted earlier that I have explored problems about these kinds of personal attribute elsewhere (Davis, 1988, 1990, 1993, 1995, 1996a). In the light of the new material presented in this chapter I will be able to revisit these explorations now with the benefit of a richer background of argument. A simple distinction needs outlining before I can proceed.

We may distinguish between *token* activities or tasks, and *types*. Jane makes a tower with her bricks on Thursday morning. Not content with this, she makes a similar tower on Friday afternoon. Here we have two distinct token activities, which are uniquely identifiable by the time and place of their occurrences. We could also refer to a *type* activity — making towers from bricks — of which each token activity is an instance. Needless to say, the activities will have many other properties, some of which each token will share with the other, and others of which will differ. Perhaps Jane uses different coloured bricks on the second occasion, takes less time, gets bored, talks to a different friend about what she is doing, and so forth. The token-type distinction cannot be applied to 'topics' or 'subject matters'. Perhaps we could talk of two (token) topics of the Romans, one being studied in Puddletown Primary and the other at Gas Lane Primary, but this has a strange ring to it. Topics and subject matters are abstractions, whose very 'natures' are defined by their non-relational, or 'intrinsic', properties.

As we saw in Chapter 3, we can invent properties to go with any of the descriptions we apply to objects, activities, tasks, topics, subject matters, and so on. (I allow myself here to make references to properties as though they can be identified as discrete items. But this is for expository purposes only.) If I say truthfully: 'This chair is the one my aunt gave to her cousin in 1957', then it seems but a small transition to announce that this chair has the property of having been given by my aunt to her cousin in 1957. Or again: 'the chair is wooden' goes with the idea that the chair has the property of being wooden. It is clear that there is a substantial difference, however, between the first and the second examples. The property of being wooden is something 'intrinsic' to the chair. The property of being given by my aunt to her cousin is a 'relational' property; objective enough, yet it is a matter of the connections between the chair and a couple of people, rather than of the qualities peculiar to the chair itself.

'Relational' properties are not the only types of properties that seem to have less to do with the item itself than something 'external' to it. In our discussion of the situated cognition tradition, and elsewhere, we have seen that action properties present a particularly rich field in this respect. Suppose Jones throws a brick. 'Jones broke the window' attributes a 'property' to his act, but the description of the action is in terms of a result. This description can be equally apt, whether or not Jones intended the outrage. At the same time, if the breaking of the window was not intended, the property attributed seems somehow to be external to that act. As we have seen, actions also attract descriptions in virtue of conforming to conventions, or as exemplifying aspects of complex conceptual schemes possessed by the community. Moving the knight just so was a move in a game of chess. It may well count as a move, whether or not Jones intended it. However, if he did it in an absent-minded fit but his stern opponent still insists that it must count, its 'property' of being a chess move seems not to be intrinsic to it.

There seem to be strong analogies here with the issue of reporting beliefs discussed in an earlier chapter. When Jones intends to break the window, or intends his activity with the knight to be a proper move, then our reports that he broke the window, or moved his knight, correspond with *de dicto* belief reports. When Jones did not intend the window disaster, and fiddled absent-mindedly with the chess piece, but is still reported as breaking the window, or moving the knight, such reporting seems to echo the *de re* reporting of beliefs.

Notions of abilities, traits, competencies and so on are intimately linked to act types. I am able to slice vegetables. This presumably means that I can perform any number of act tokens which may be appropriately classified as slicing vegetables. No one act of slicing will precisely resemble another. We can with propriety award each act other properties, such as being the first job with the new knife, helping to make the stew, using my aunt's chopping board, and so forth. For any act type we can invent a capacity, ability or skill to accompany it. Consider the following four act tokens: Jim mends his gutter, replaces the fuse in the vacuum cleaner, cleans the sparking plug in the Fiesta and oils the stiff lock on the garage door. Each of these is a piece of practical problem-solving. Each of them possesses the property of practical problem solving, or belongs to the act-type solving a practical problem. In the light of these, we might say that Jim has a practical problem-solving ability (Davis, 1988).

It is possible that these kinds of ability expressions are used on occasion simply to summarise previous achievements. Or again, we may by ascribing a practical problem-solving ability to someone intend to draw attention to personality traits which are not essentially cognitive. We might want to talk about Jim's customary enthusiasm for practical tasks, the way he always sets about them immediately, finishes what he has started, and so on. Where we merely summarise previous achievements, the shift to ability or competence talk is superficial and harmless. In cases where we are gesturing at attitude and motivation, the collection of act tokens may be thought to be evidence of these attitudes. There seems to be no objection to such a move. Jim's series of successes at solving practical problems might well, together with other circumstances, amount to a justification for attributing certain attitudes to him.

Now it is very clear that much ability and skill talk is intended to go well beyond this. Pupils are supposed to acquire abilities related to numeracy and literacy which transfer to employment contexts. It is believed to be possible for them to come to possess a stable underlying trait which can persist over a period of time, and which will enable us to predict success in a range of future circumstances. This does not imply that if an ability can be possessed it can only be possessed 'in full'.

The model behind this type of trait language reminds us once more of some aspects of the powers and dispositions conceptual scheme when applied to physical substances, which was discussed at length in Chapter 4. Now the majority of abilities referred to in educational contexts, those for instance featured within literacy and numeracy, or those expected of pupils in the National Curriculum (e.g. 'Pupils carry through substantial tasks and solve quite complex problems by breaking them down into smaller, more manageable tasks', DFE, 1995b, p. 23), involve multi-track dispositions with a vengeance.

As we saw when comparing dispositional aspects of belief with the powers and dispositions of substances, something is required to bind the disparate phenomena which may figure in multi-track dispositions such as being magnetic. In the case of the latter, the underlying state explaining magnetic phenomena involves the arrangement of atoms and electrons. This binding provides the necessary support for referring to a variety of phenomena as manifestations of magnetism, even though the range of behaviour covered by magnetism is relatively circumscribed. If we seek for analogous 'binding' to unite and explain the range of behaviour which may be covered by many human abilities, unease of two different types is likely to surface.

Unease of the first kind is empirical. What could justify our confidence, for instance, that we could predict a child's success in the almost infinite diversity of behaviour which might be taken as 'doing additions' on the basis of her performance in a few kinds of contexts involving sweets, pictures and counting?

Winch and Gingell (1996) criticised me for apparently denying the 'plasticity' of abilities. On their interpretation, denying that abilities are 'plastic' amounts to denying that we can predict on the basis of success in a given context that the same success will be gained in further contexts. They observe:

> If someone succeeds in performing an emergency stop on Acacia Avenue in the course of his driving test, we are prepared to accept that he will be able to perform an emergency stop on most, if not all other roads. If he is able to read *The Lion, the Witch and the Wardrobe* successfully, then it is safe to assume that he will be able to read *The Hobbit* and various other books (p. 380).

In their sense of 'plastic' I would not deny that abilities are (sometimes) plastic. Winch and Gingell were not accusing me, I think, of a failure to accept inductive argument. They were concerned rather that I placed too great an emphasis on the particularity of the context in which a given performance took place. They felt that I was guilty of this failing to such an extent that I believed there was no good reason for making any predictions about 'relevant' future performances.

In the end as I say this is an empirical issue. Nevertheless it should be observed that they take as unproblematic the ways in which contexts and actions may be said to resemble or to differ from each other. 'There is no good reason to think that practical contexts are sufficiently different from assessment situations so that knowledge will not be properly measured' (*ibid.*, pp. 380–1).

At the empirical level we may note that there is much evidence to the effect that people do not always perform in the 'same' way in 'similar' contexts. APU surveys pointed up how trivial differences in task or context apparently made large differences to performance levels. Verdicts from research into the extent to which more general abilities such as problem-solving skills 'transfer' is far from positive (Detterman, 1993). My impression, based on anecdotal evidence only, suggests that there is the least difficulty about 'plasticity' when the abilities concerned are relatively unsaturated with rich declarative knowledge. Consider the 'ability' to run 100 metres in a given time, which seems very likely to 'transfer' to performance over 120 metres, or the 'ability' to sing middle C, which should transfer to the production of the E above middle C. Many of the abilities which turn out to be genuinely plastic are physical, and may be characterised quite precisely in observable terms.

A deeper unease associated with the search for something to 'bind' disparate behaviour into abilities or competencies relates to the challenges and complexities we have been investigating about similarity. Act typologies, as we have seen, often reflect aspects of context and social institutions, in addition to the consequences of events which we import back to the action description after the event. For instance, at the time we said that Jones *threw the ball*, but later we said that he *broke the window*, arguably on each occasion character-ising one and the same action. In what could the identity over time of many traits of a more complex cognitive character possibly consist?

Much trait terminology is to some degree mythological. The terminology remains in good health for a number of reasons. I mention three here. First, there is the fact that human performance does exhibit some degree of plasticity, even though the form this takes is actually quite difficult to predict except in the case of very simple skills. Second, there is the ease with which we can create phrases which seem to refer nicely to traits, e.g. caring skills, the ability to write to suit a particular audience, or spatial ability. Third, it is very convenient to imagine that we can assess a pupil for the presence of a trait now, which later will stand her in good stead in the workplace or in adult life generally.

To sum up, we are often unable to identify independently from particular social contexts individual cognitive traits or competencies which may be thought of as persisting over time and manifestable in a range of future circumstances. These difficulties arise with particular force in respect of some achievements and contexts with which education concerns itself.

PSYCHOMETRICS AND TRAITS

In a previous paper (Davis, 1993) I asked whether psychometrics could help with the problems about identifying and reidentifying cognitive traits over time. After all, workers in this tradition make free and confident use of terms such as 'spatial ability', 'general intelligence' and 'verbal ability'. The impression is given that they not only know what they are referring to, but have reason to think that they can communicate clearly with others about a shared subject-matter. While it is true that psychometrics does not seek to deal with the complex ability attributions which are common in educational contexts, yet if the tradition can solve the problem in conceptually simpler cases we can surely learn from their success. Or so it might be argued.

It is standard in this tradition to infer the existence of abilities or traits from the fact that certain test results correlate. I now outline an artificially simple case in order to make a point, without for a moment suggesting that real instances would be as crude as this. Suppose we have one test which purports to scrutinise pupils' English, and a second which is supposed to assess their arithmetic. The initial move is to say that the first test probes an ability in English, while the second examines an ability in arithmetic. If the results of using the English test on a number of pupils correlate very highly with the results of using the arithmetic test on the same pupils, it is customary in this field to claim that the two tests are sampling the 'same' ability, despite the probable intentions of the test constructors. If the English test results in no way correlate with the arithmetic test results, it is equally standard to urge that they are measuring 'different' abilities.

In the light of earlier discussion of ideas of sameness, similarity and transfer, it is only too clear that psychometrics is not going to be able to help. The trouble begins right at the beginning, when the test items are selected. As I wrote in an earlier paper (Davis, 1993):

> We have had to set up a system of CATEGORIES or KINDS of performances when we devise our tests in the first place. For a test to count as an arithmetic test, we must have in mind a class of performances which resemble each other in respect of being instances of 'doing arithmetic'. For a later administration of a test to count as giving the 'same test', where we do not literally repeat the same items, we require a clear conception of 'item kinds' which allows us to devise a 'comparable' test.

It would be futile to attack the human practices of making judgements about tasks and of deciding which are similar and which are different. Such customs are perfectly healthy, and I have not sought to show that they are defective. Yet we know that pupils can respond very differently to test items apparently as a result of very small differences between the items. The APU provided splendid data of this kind (for a good summary see Cambridge Institute of

Education, 1985). The crucial point here is that we seem to have a choice about how these differences may be explained.

Item 'similarity' may simply be assumed. In that case, it will be suggested that divergences in responses are due to certain kinds of misunderstandings, varying reading difficulties, distractions arising from change of layout, and so on. The trouble is that we can equally well turn the story on its head. We can say that where there are no very obvious features of this kind, the differences in responses show that the items are not actually similar to each other even if at first sight they seemed to be. We can even go as far as saying that items which look very different from each other, if producing highly correlated responses, are really 'very similar' or 'the same'. There seems to be no ultimate rational ground on which we can choose between these alternative ways of running the explanation.

This is bad news for any hope that psychometrics might assist us with the problem of transfer and traits. The whole point concerning worries about transfer in education is that people often cannot perform adequately in contexts seemingly demanding a similar competence or area of knowledge to one they already possess. Psychometrics cannot clarify the nature of 'mental muscles', even if they exist. It does not provide us with a coherent account of *kinds* of actions of which agents would be repeatedly capable if they possessed the relevant capacities.

MATHEMATICAL PERFORMANCES AND SIMILARITY JUDGEMENTS: WHAT 'THEORY' INFORMS THEM?

I want to return now to a further consideration of Goodman's idea that similarity judgements require some kind of *theory*. Its application to mathematical performances will enable many of the arguments in this chapter to be driven home.

The socially constructed set of concepts called mathematics might be referred to as 'theory', and certainly provides us with a perspective from which we judge 3 − 8 to be relevantly similar to other more straightforward instances of subtraction. It is essential to remember at this point that mathematics 'exists' within the adult community as a social activity (Ernest, 1991) rather than within the mind of any one individual. Some individuals know rather more mathematics than others. Children in varying degrees own plenty of bad mathematics. They will believe in false mathematical propositions, imagine concepts to be necessarily connected when they are entirely distinct, and fail to discern necessary connections. In short, they will not be in possession of that full theoretical perspective from which 3 − 8 may be judged to be relevantly similar to other more straightforward instances of subtraction.

If we couch the learning of mathematics in the discourse of situated learning, we may offer observations of this kind: pupils will learn the practice of mathematics mainly by engaging in mathematical activities, especially with others who have a richer grasp of the version of the subject currently extant in the community. They will, for instance, gradually come to know that a diverse range of processes or operations may be regarded as similar in certain respects and hence classified as subtractions. This apprenticeship will always be incomplete. The child will have to learn that in this context answering $2 - 5$ by deploying negative numbers, and interpreting the symbol '$-$' as counting backwards on a number line, is still thought of as subtraction. Certainly, when the child participates in a range of social activities of a mathematical character she will gradually acquire notions of similarity held by the mathematical community.

However, the pupil can never acquire a conception of similarity such that it could be regarded as settled in advance, so to speak, whether any hitherto uncontemplated process or operation, detached from its social situation, should be classified as a subtraction. The notion of matters being settled in advance in this way is incoherent. No relevant community can in principle shape this thought.

To see this, we may imagine an agent asking: 'Is this action (situation, process, operation) the same again? For instance, is it in fact another subtraction?' The complexity of this thought experiment should not be underestimated. To what item, precisely, is the phrase 'this action' supposed to refer? What properties has the agent already assigned to it in thought in order to refer to it in her mind? Is she merely thinking of a physical movement? For instance, does she conceive of those steps backwards as part of a game, moves along a number line she pretends is underfoot, or an exercise to rid herself of cramp? There is the further question of which objective physical properties the action possesses, regardless of how the agent sees her performance. If, for instance, she takes a few steps backwards then her action is certainly at least those physical movements, leaving aside any other properties it may possess.

Whatever her mathematical theory, which might inform her judgements about similarity, there is a host of unpredictable variables here to do with the 'situatedness' of the performance being considered. These will affect her final verdict on the problem of whether the action is the same again.

The community will also have a view about whether her action is the same again. The judgements of the community are situated within their culture, practices, beliefs, values and conceptions of mathematics. The 'theory' which might be said to evaluate similarity judgements made about mathematical performances is mathematics as socially constructed and having an existence within social institutions, socially sustained conventions, and so on. Yet whether the pupil will succeed on a task of a particular kind, given past successes, depends crucially upon whether *she* sees her current action and situation as relevantly similar. As a mere individual, and more particularly as a pupil, she will not be in complete possession of 'mathematics'. Her similarity judgements will inevitably diverge to some extent from those of the adult community.

It follows that we cannot in principle identify something within the child, a 'subtraction competence', which could ground success in the range of performances and situations which we might judge to be subtractions in the light of our current mathematical 'theory'. We can only speak more loosely about her successes in activities which both she and we are inclined to call subtraction, and possibly in the light of this exhibit a more diffuse optimism about future performance on 'similar' subtractions. We need to be clear that this way of talking and of thinking is imprecise, and cannot be tightened up.

Undoubtedly some of our established action classifications endure because agents successful in one instance tend to be successful at others within the same classification. Perhaps pupils successful on one kind of 'subtraction' do tend to triumph on seemingly very different 'subtractions'. Incidentally, empirical research evidence about mathematics learning is decidedly equivocal on this point: see Ruthven (1988). Nevertheless generally speaking we are often in principle unable to be precise about the nature of our classifications of current pupil successes. We are in a similar position in respect of the different categories of performance to which current competence might be thought to transfer.

IS ARITHMETIC A SPECIAL CASE? IS THE ARGUMENT DISTORTED BY THE USE OF UNREPRESENTATIVE EXAMPLES?

It may be objected that much of the discussion has made use of mathematical examples. Through this narrow range of examples have I perhaps loaded the odds against transfer as something about which we can be precise, and with reference to which we can make specific predictions about pupil or adult performance?

I would respond that the role of social definition of 'similarity' in connection with such alleged capacities as listening skills, thinking skills, observation skills, problem-solving skills and communication skills is very substantial. Undoubtedly the discourse in which we characterise mathematical attainments will have some distinctive features which mark them off from scientific, literary or artistic achievements. However it is difficult to see how and why such distinctiveness should be connected with special difficulties about transfer.

At least arithmetic concepts and their applications are bonded together by logical relationships. This might be thought to justify a degree of *optimism* to the effect that once pupils have learned the adult mathematical concept network their judgements about the sameness of activities will approach those of the community more generally. If $3-8$ were *not* judged to be subtraction, this would have implications for the rest of arithmetic. For instance, it would influence our conception of $8-3$. One legitimate way in which the latter is regarded is by means of a number line. $8-3$ can be interpreted to mean that three moves should be made from 8 in the direction of zero along a number line. Without $3-8$ as subtraction, this would be ruled out, or restricted to the natural numbers. The idea of number itself would be restricted to countable items and measurable quantities.

Compare the situation regarding arithmetic attainments with that pertaining to attainments in English, design, religious education, art or working in a team. Here, judgements that the pupil is acting *in the same way again* will invariably involve concepts lacking comprehensive logical interconnections. Admittedly the situation in science is sometimes closer to that which prevails in mathematics: some systems of concepts are at least locally connected, as are force, mass and acceleration in Newtonian mechanics.

Much space has been devoted to the kind of knowledge and competence the transfer of which resists precise analysis. The point also needs to be made that in the case of certain carefully selected candidates the case for transfer may be stronger. These are cases where the idea of underlying traits seems more plausible. To search for these candidates we must bear in mind the concerns about the notion of similarity which have beset the typical complex cognitive capacities fostered within educational institutions.

Some so-called physical skills seem to survive the critique of this chapter. Consider Jones's putative ability to throw a ball. It seems straightforward to define a category of arm movements and resulting ball movements to which actions would need to conform to manifest this ability. Here we have laid down ways in which current actions should resemble past actions to count as manifestations of the 'same' ability. Because the properties of the actions concerned are physically defined, they may be detached from their contexts. Their identity is stipulated physically. Further, it is not implausible to suppose that there are some underlying states of Jones's brain, musculature, and so on, which persist over time, which could be identified and re-identified, and which explain that he throws a ball when he chooses, other things being equal.

However, even in this area we should be cautious about identifying abilities too readily. Unless the skills concerned are very primitive and physical in character, they are likely to involve more 'rich' knowledge than is immediately apparent, bringing in at least some of the complexities stemming from social definitions of identity and similarity already discussed.

Whatever conclusions are finally reached about these apparently more robust skills, much of the pupil attainment in which the state wishes to interest itself through assessment is not of this kind. However, in addition to 'thin' physical skills, it may be thought there are mental skills of certain types which can be detached from contexts and thus escape the critique of this chapter. I have in mind what might be characterised as algorithmic skills, and will discuss them towards the end of the chapter.

WITTGENSTEINIAN RULE-FOLLOWING CONSIDERATIONS

My current argument owes something to Wittgenstein's treatment of rule-following. Accordingly I turn to a brief discussion of that treatment in this section. In the next section I draw attention to a global sceptical argument that has been thought to derive from the rule-following considerations. I compare and contrast it with my treatment of rule-following and similarity when applied to human performances and their contexts.

For Wittgenstein, following a rule was bound up with the idea of doing the same thing again. 'I have . . . indicated that a person goes by a sign-post only in so far as there exists a regular use of sign-posts, a custom' (Wittgenstein, 1958, p. 80); 'The use of the word "rule" and the use of the word "same" are interwoven' (*ibid.*).

Teachers may think that part of their task is to impart rules to their pupils which they can eventually use in a wide range of contexts. The mastery of the right kind of rule, it may seem, will enable pupils to transfer their learning from familiar to less familiar situations.

In a justly famous treatment of rule-following considerations Kripke (1982) was struck by what he took to be an important set of arguments when reading Wittgenstein. He declined the role of interpreter altogether, discussed 'arguments which occurred to Kripke while reading Wittgenstein', and did not claim exegetical accuracy of any kind. This approach also seems very appropriate in a book about educational assessment. I am trying to communicate with those interested in learning and in education policy, rather than Wittgenstein scholars. Hence, if you choose, substitute 'Wittgenstein' (scare quotes) for Wittgenstein in the following. Initially I lean on Baker and Hacker (1985), especially pp. 154 ff.

Wittgenstein does not think that meaning can exist independently of rules. Hence he sees an investigation into conceptions of rules as crucial. For him, speaking a language is engaging in a range of contextualised rule-governed activities. It would make no sense to describe two persons as playing chess (or following the rules of chess) if they belonged to a culture unacquainted with games. 'It is only against a certain complex background that acting in accord with a rule counts as following the rule' (Baker and Hacker, 1985, p. 159).

Rule-following requires the existence of an established use or custom. Understanding a rule is to possess certain abilities. Wittgenstein distinguishes between following a rule, where an agent 'knows that there is a rule, understands it, and intentionally moulds his actions to it' (1958, p. 155), and merely acting in accord with a rule, as a monkey might move pieces on a chess board in a way which happened to conform with the rules.

The notion of 'the same again' is tied to the nature of the practice in question. The rule determines what counts as the same.

Is adding 15 to 27 doing something different from adding 15 to 68? The numbers added to 15 are different and so are the results. But one can also say that one does the same thing to 27 as one then does to 68, viz one adds 15 to it. And one might well say that one does the same thing to a pair of numbers in adding 15 to 68 as one does in adding 89 to 72, viz one calculates their sum (as opposed to their difference or product). These uses of 'doing the same' are severally legitimate; they are not in conflict. Bewilderment arises from thinking that there must, in such cases, be a single, correct, context-free, purpose-independent answer to the question of whether this is doing the same as that (*ibid.*, p. 166).

Baker and Hacker suggest that Wittgenstein distinguished between applying a fixed technique to new cases, and extending a technique to a new domain. They contend that such a distinction is robust and principled even if it may be difficult on occasion to assign a given example to the appropriate category. An instance of applying a fixed technique is given as multiplying pairs of natural numbers, and it is claimed that its applicability is independent of the size of the numbers. Extending a technique is exemplified by allowing multiplication for signed integers and then extending it to rational, irrational and other kinds of numbers. 'Here . . . what is to count as "the same" must be laid down afresh and is not predetermined in the antecedent technique' (Baker and Hacker, 1985, p. 168).

If Wittgenstein did distinguish in this way between applying a fixed technique and extending a technique this move is questionable. The judgement that a domain is 'different' and hence that it requires the extending of an existing technique looks as though it will be relative to the context, interests and purposes of those making the judgement. Applying a 'fixed technique' looks as though it is linked to a notion of analyticity, for which Wittgenstein would have little sympathy given his account of similarity as family resemblance.

Wittgenstein is credited with the view that there is no context-free notion of similarity to which we can appeal when following a rule. If accepted, this supports the thesis defended so far in this chapter, according to which there is no context-free notion of similarity which can be applied to actions, contexts, or most of the phenomena associated with cognitive achievement. However, I am further arguing that the status of sameness and similarity judgements varies depending on whether the subject matter is human activity or physical or chemical phenomena. A defensible 'realism' for chemistry supports robust similarity judgements which are not available in human contexts.

RULE-FOLLOWING CONSIDERATIONS AND A POSSIBLE SCEPTICAL ARGUMENT

I want now to mention a very general sceptical position which Kripke associates with rule-following considerations. Some might mistakenly interpret my claims about similarity and transfer to stem from such a global perspective. On that basis, my arguments might be rejected as examples of mere philosophical doubt, in the same spirit that we are disposed to reject Cartesian or Humean doubt.

It has been argued (Sklar, 1980) that we can use a predicate even in a sentence whose truth condition we are unable to recognise as obtaining 'by analogy' with the sense which that predicate has in other sentences whose truth conditions we can recognise as obtaining.

Yet a sceptic may find a difficulty with the notion of 'analogy' here. It relies on the seemingly uncontentious assumption that a given predicate 'is P' can have a particular sense or meaning, in its occurrence in the utterance of a particular speaker on a particular occasion, and that the speaker can transfer this sense to a new sentence. The assumption may seem not only uncontentious, but essential to account for speakers' capacities to produce and understand a potentially infinite number of sentences with the resources of a finite set of components. (This point was referred to in Chapter 3 as involved in Dummett's objection to meaning holism.) We are compelled, of course, to accept that speakers do possess such a capacity. It is when we come to elucidate this capacity that the problems begin.

Let us attempt a common-sense description of this capacity before noting the sceptic's challenge. A speaker encounters a sentence S containing the predicate 'is P'. He comes to understand this sentence. In particular, he understands '— is P'. What he understands is that the predicate is applicable to something just when that something possesses the property P. Hence he can understand the meaning of ' — is P' even if it occurs in a new sentence whose meaning as a whole is such that he cannot acquire or manifest an understanding of it. The speaker will think that to understand what it is like for something to be P in the new or previously unencountered context, he must remember what it is like for the subject of S to be P and perform an act of analogical transfer.

The sceptic can claim that the above description depicts the situation the wrong way round. According to him, individually and as a community we just do apply 'is P' in new situations. But our applications of '— is P' in fresh instances are not as they are because we discern manifestations of the property P in new situations. It is rather that we say that the property P is manifested on the new occasion as a consequence of our decision to apply the predicate '— is P' to that new situation.

The common-sense description suggested that we apply the same predicate because we discern the same property. The sceptical view is that we can only make sense of the fresh situation involving a manifestation of the same property as a result of, or consequential upon, our deciding to apply the same predicate '— is P' in the new situation as we did in the old.

Kripke presents his argument for the sceptical view by means of a mathematical example. English-speakers use 'plus' and ' + ' to denote addition. On the orthodox account of what it is to know the meaning of 'plus' or ' + ' as an English speaker I have grasped a rule. The application of this rule determines my answer for indefinitely many new sums that I have never performed before (Kripke, 1982). Suppose that '68 + 57' is a new computation for me. I perform it and obtain 125. I think that this is both arithmetically and metalinguistically correct. 'Plus', as I intended to use the word in the past, denoted a function which, when applied to the numbers I called '68' and '57', yields the value of 125.

Suppose someone suggests that, as I used 'plus' in the past, the answer I intended for 68 + 57 should have been 5. I attempt to reject the suggestion by saying that I am following the rule I followed on previous occasions. The difficulty now arises in determining what that rule was, since I can only have thought of a finite number of applications of it. Perhaps, the sceptic suggests, I used 'plus' and ' + '

in the past to denote a function which I will call 'quus' and symbolise by @. It is defined by: $x @ y = x + y$, if x, y, < 57. Otherwise $x @ y = 5$.

Though I would of course reject this extraordinary proposal, and would be 'right' to do so, it is not facts about my past usage that compel or justify the answer 125 rather than 5. Nor is it a matter of instructions I gave myself in the past. *Ex hypothesi* the computation '68 + 57' is not included in such facts or instructions.

How are we elucidate our common-sense notion that our present usage conforms to our previous usage, i.e. that we are following the same rule as we did in the past? What happened in the past can come under an indefinite variety of descriptions. Apparently it could be supposed in turn that an indefinite variety of rules were being followed. Hence we cannot say that the answer '5' is wrong on the basis of 'facts' about previous usage of 'plus' or ' + ' of the form: I followed such and such a rule for the use of 'plus' or ' + '.

These considerations are not peculiar to mathematical examples. For instance, I think perhaps that I know the rule for the use of 'table' so that I can apply the expression to indefinitely many future items. I might then hold that it is settled in advance on the basis of my grasp of the rule for 'table' that the term in question would apply to a table found at the base of the Eiffel Tower. But before I actually go to the Tower, and employ, or fail to employ, the expression, is its applicability really settled in advance by my previous usage? My previous usage might be said by a sceptic to be as follows. In the past by 'table' I meant *tabair*, where a 'tabair' is anything that is a table not found at the base of the Eiffel Tower, or a chair found there.

The version of rule-following scepticism outlined here does not attempt to establish that there is no sense whatever to the thought that matters are in some fashion 'settled in advance'. It rather attempts to establish that matters cannot be settled in advance by previous usage according to a rule framed in a particular way. The style of rule framing under attack is exemplified by: *Apply '— is a table' just when the property of being a table is manifested.*

There is nothing epistemological about these arguments. The problem is not: how do I know that I am following the same rule now as I did in the past? It is rather: what does it mean to say that I am following the *same rule* for my current action as I followed with certain of my past actions? For any number of rules may be formulated which could fit my previous actions.

These arguments resemble Goodman's in some ways, but they are so general that they are too true to be good. If they are accepted they apply to any situations in which I make judgements about sameness or similarity over time. My concern is that their very universality might seem to undermine my contentions about transfer, which are of course specific to human actions, undertakings and contexts. Kripke's Wittgenstein is mentioned here, then, in order to be discarded. In the same spirit, it will be recalled, problems about induction and about the functioning of vague predicates were mentioned earlier in the chapter, in order to set them on one side. The strictures on similarity which I am pursuing in connection with judgements about human performances, knowledge and contexts must be sharply distinguished from any very general scepticism which may be thought to be derivable from the rule-following considerations.

RULES REVISITED

It may be objected at this point that although much has been said about rules I have failed to do justice to their simple power. My critique of transfer must be flawed since we make constant use of rules in different contexts. They are powerful and practical devices. Following these rules involves knowing exactly what they mean. Hence, this objection concludes, not only does following a rule facilitate transfer but an inspection of it enables us to be quite precise about the forms in which the transfer will be achieved. Indeed, if someone successfully follows a rule it is hard to see why a corresponding trait or ability cannot be identified in a clear and robust fashion.

My response to this objection will ultimately involve argument of much the same kind as that deployed against trait thinking. First, let us consider a range of rules which our objector might have in mind.

- Punctuation rules. For instance: *Names begin with capital letters.*
- Spelling: *Plurals of words ending in y use -ies except . . .*
- Fractions: *To divide one fraction by another, turn the divisor fraction upside down and multiply the two fractions.*
- Part of a set of procedures for solving mathematical problems Burton, 1984):
    1.1 *Explore the problem*
    1.2 *Make and test guesses*
    1.3 *Define terms and relationships*
    1.4 *Extract information*
    1.5 *Organise the information*
    1.6 *Introduce a representation*
    1.7 *Introduce a form of recording.*
- Lawn mowing: *Do not cut the grass when it is wet.*

We can invent abilities to go with the rules, such as the capacity to use capitals in connection with names, to divide fractions, to solve mathematical problems, and the like. All the candidate rules are framed in words, and I will assume for the sake of argument that all allegedly 'powerful' rules can be expressed verbally.

John Searle's (1992) views about what he calls 'the Background', if correct, have important implications for the viability of rules as tools for transfer. He attributes the idea of 'the Background' to Wittgenstein, and indeed there are echoes in what has already been said about rule-following. To explain the idea, he provides a series of examples in which the 'same literal expression makes the same contribution to the literal utterance of a variety of sentences, and yet . . . the expression will be interpreted differently in the different sentences . . . each sentence is interpreted against a Background of human capacities (abilities to engage in certain practices, know-how, ways of doing things, etc.), and those capacities will fix different interpretations, even though the literal meaning of the expression remains constant' (p. 179).

He invites us to consider occurrences of 'cut' in 'Sam cut the grass', 'Sam cut the cake', 'Bill cut the cloth', 'I just cut my skin'. He insists that all these occurrences are literal, inviting us if in any doubt to compare them with 'Sally cut two classes last week' or 'The president cut the salaries of the professors', where it is quite clear that 'cut' is used metaphorically. He also insists that each *literal* use of cut is interpreted differently. The point is brought out forcefully by considering the possibility that when someone is told to cut the grass they rush out and stab it with a knife, or when required to cut the cake they run over it with a lawn mower.

It is never possible, he continues, to make matters more precise to ensure total explicitness and to rule out all possibility of misinterpretation. The man in the restaurant orders a meal, saying 'Bring me a steak with fried potatoes'. It is taken for granted that the food will not be delivered to the man's home or place of work. The steak will not be encased in concrete, stuffed into his pockets or placed on his head. If we try to rule out these possibilities with further instructions, this simply brings into play a whole new set of possible misinterpretations which themselves would have to be discouraged by further verbal qualifications.

When we have a rule expressed in words, we have the idea that its application in future cases is fixed. Now evidently many rules do provide us with a guide to future action. If we take Searle's contentions seriously, this guide is conditional upon the Background. Each particular implementation of the rule must be interpreted in its context, just as the sentences including 'cut' were construed as expressing a diverse range of thoughts depending on their context. The Background includes the regularity with which the physical world behaves, and our knowledge of it, together with human capacities, dispositions, ways of behaving, know-how, and so on. (When summarising the nature of the background, Searle does not mention the law-governed behaviour of the physical world, though it features prominently in his discussion of examples.)

Searle does not see the identity over time of human capacities and dispositions as in any way problematic. Now I believe that he is right not to question the existence of patterns of human behaviour. What is 'problematic', as we have seen, is what is to count as *the same trait over time*. In the case of many cognitive capacities, it is not possible in principle to establish clear identity criteria. To appeal to the notion of a rule to paper over the cracks we have uncovered in the idea of transfer is to appeal to something which itself depends on the Background. Yet it would not be possible to codify the way in which the Background impinges on the interpretation of the rule in a particular context in order to deliver a robust account of the rule in which all its implementations were transparent and somehow built into its intrinsic meaning. We could not usefully and conclusively supplement the rule with instructions on how it should be interpreted in various contexts, since these would themselves be subject to interpretation via the operation of the Background.

Let us think this through by making use of an example. Consider the rule that a full stop should be used at the end of a sentence, followed by a capital letter to begin the next sentence. The related ability or competence was unpacked a little in Chapter 2, and turned out to involve practical know-how strongly suffused with rich declarative knowledge. When discussed at that stage, it was referred to as though it was reasonably clear what it would mean for such a competence to exist. The idea of an identifiable competence of a stable character, persisting over time, and explaining successful performances with full stops and capital letters in a wide range of contexts, was assumed to be coherent. Jones today enters information in a database (and quite possibly refrains from applying standard punctuation conventions). In Chapter 2 we spoke as though it made perfectly good sense to think of Jones as exercising the *same competence* today as that which he developed at school.

When constructing a spelling test, or constructing an index for a book, I may well decline to use full stops and capital letters in the traditional fashion. I could have excellent reasons for setting aside punctuation conventions. The way I lay out an index might well manifest my competence with capital letters and full stops, even though I fail to punctuate 'normally', since I deliberately choose not to follow customary practice.

However, my index format could hardly be said to be an implementation of the rule that a full stop should be used at the end of a sentence, followed by a capital letter to begin the next sentence. I suggest that this point is one symptom of the difficulty we are likely to encounter if we think that a straightforward implementation of the punctuation rule will achieve transfer. The rule requires much other knowledge for appropriate application. It is far from being mechanical or algorithmic, and the wise user will in some contexts deliberately refrain from implementing it. Its interpretation will vary considerably, depending on which aspects of the Background impinge on any proposed application.

Should the rule protagonist now give up? Before he does, let us credit him with a possible counter move. He might argue that the role of the Background can be set to one side if we frame a much more tightly focused rule about punctuation than that just discussed. For instance, instead of a general rule about capital letters and full stops purportedly applicable in an indefinite variety of contexts, we could frame a rule about what to do when presented by the teacher with prose passages omitting punctuation. Pupils would be asked to detect complete sentences, to place full stops at their ends and to capitalise the beginnings of the following sentences.

Given a manoeuvre of this kind, we apparently have a rule with a transparent identity and unambiguous application. However, this manoeuvre achieves much less than might have first appeared. In future applications the prose will need to be of comparable difficulty and length, the time allowed for the exercise the same, the atmosphere the same and the teacher direction on each occasion similar. When I say that the Background can be set to one side I am not implying that it is now no longer an essential framework enabling the rule follower to 'decode' the instruction she is giving to herself. The point I am making is that the Background is, so to speak, being held constant from one performance to the next. We are 'cheating'. We have not simply invented a new rule. We have tried to supplement it by controlling the background conditions for its interpretation. This in effect prevents the rule from being applicable in a variety of circumstances.

Have we been unfair to the rule theorist, and lurched from one extreme to the other? Is this fresh rule now narrowly focused in an absurd manner? After all, it would be much more 'practical' if for instance it could somehow be extended to cover the ways in which people should punctuate their own free writing. This, it might be urged, is still covering the 'same' area. The latter thought may stem from a conviction that success with teacher exercises and with personally generated writing obviously derives from the *same* competence.

My response is that it would be difficult now to invent a rule expressible in words to cover this range of performance and circumstances. Even if this could be done, the Background can no longer be controlled. Remember the claim at the heart of this chapter, namely that judgements about sameness are context-bound. Considered properly, this undermines the idea that 'one' punctuation competence could be involved. It destroys any claim that employing the right kinds of rules could underpin significant instances of transfer.

ALGORITHMS

Some will feel that the potential of rule-following for facilitating an explication of and confidence in precise transfer has still not been properly exploited. Another category of examples which might be offered would be that of algorithms. Again, mathematics is the most obvious source for paradigms. Some of us can still do long division, whether or not we understand our own actions. If we go through a series of steps accurately, we will be able to divide numbers regardless of size and decimal places. These steps may be thought of as 'mechanical', and indeed the very 'same' steps can be implemented on a computer by means of an appropriate programme. Early in the section, we mentioned part of an algorithm for dividing fractions; the steps to be taken after we had turned upside down and multiplied were not specified, but they could be in detail if required.

In rejecting algorithmic thinking as a possible support for transfer, it should not be assumed that I despise this type of thinking as such. On the contrary, it can be extremely useful. Those best placed to deploy it to maximum advantage have a background of proper knowledge about the area to which algorithmic rules apply. They can lift off, so to speak, from a mode of operating relying on relational understanding, implement algorithms with efficiency, and then apply the result back in subject matters and contexts which are thoroughly understood. Chapter 2 briefly sketched this mode of operating for the 'turn upside down and multiply' rule for dividing fractions. Competent operators of this algorithm can actually work through simple cases from first principles, and thoroughly understand why it works. They operate algorithmically with complex fractions because this is efficient. But they can always return to the level of 'real understanding'.

The point has to be made, however, that operating algorithmically can be a matter of operating with little understanding. The process can be carried out fairly mechanically. Little meaning need be attached to the manipulations. Interpretations are unnecessary. No use or application has to be considered. Again then the Background is being built out of the scenario. We can now see that what has in effect been left out is, crucially, transfer itself.

WHAT FOLLOWS FROM SCEPTICISM ABOUT FINE-GRAINED TRANSFER OF COGNITIVE ACHIEVEMENT?

What conclusions may be drawn from this sceptical review of the notions of transfer and similarity? If schools are to be held to account through assessment, then either the curriculum content is justified by means of the needs of an industrial economy or it is not. If not, we may for instance appeal to the requirements of a healthy liberal democracy, or the intrinsic worthwhileness of the content, or the value of passing on a 'heritage', or the transmission of the norms and expertise of a particular culture. In the context of such requirements, transfer from school achievements to the performances of adult citizens would be needed, but in a global sense rather than in the form of specified knowledge or competence.

If the needs of an industrial economy are to the fore, then specific transfer between pupil activity and employee activity is likely to be thought of the greatest significance. It will be seen as vital that the assessment devices in place do succeed in tapping the kind of knowledge, understanding and skills which can be taken into productive adulthood.

It would be foolish to deny that there *will* be transfer between school success and employee competence. This is a matter of empirical record. However, comprehensive characterisation of such transfer in precise terms is necessarily unavailable. We may be seduced by our own language into thinking that we can pinpoint competencies or areas of knowledge and understanding, acquired at school and used in employment. Yet many of such alleged competencies cannot be unambiguously identified and re-identified over a period of time and across a range of contexts. In Chapter 2's extensive review of the conceptions of numeracy and literacy, it became clear that they would need to incorporate plenty of rich knowledge, and competencies far removed from thin skills whose identity over time is unproblematic.

Hence assessment of the basics of literacy and numeracy cannot be used in the tough, rigorous way for which governments strive in their search for accountability. We should not be pitting the effectiveness of one school against another in this fashion. For the legitimacy of so doing rests at least in part on a mythologically well-defined domain of traits, competencies and generalisable knowledge.

Chapter 7
Matching

In Chapter 1 it was noted that pupils might be assessed to enable the teacher to set tasks which were in some sense *matched* to current pupil attainment levels. I now argue that the kind of fine-grained matching thought possible by some advocating this type of assessment is a conceptual impossibility, at least in many subject areas involving any degree of cognitive complexity or challenge. The reasons for this stem from the nature of knowledge and belief as set out earlier in the book, the resistance of transfer to precise conceptualisation and the mythological nature of much of our educational discourse about cognitive traits. I have already explored ideas about matching at some length (Davis, 1993). Some of that material is further developed here. The conclusion raises significant questions about the organisa-tion of the learning of groups containing pupils with a range of attainment, and these will also be discussed.

The DES commented:

> It is not easy even for experienced teachers to match the widely differing needs and capabilities of individual children with appropriate objectives, methods and materials. In most classes, irrespective of their size, content and pace are geared to the middle level of ability in the class: able pupils are insufficiently stretched and waste time practising skills already mastered, while the diverse individual weaknesses of the less able, even when they have been diagnosed, are not tackled appropriately (1985, para. 20).

They also observed: 'There should be careful differentiation: what is taught and how it is taught need to be matched to pupils' abilities and aptitudes. It is of the greatest importance to stimulate and challenge all pupils, including the most and least able' (para. 40).

No explanation of 'matching' is supplied. Had they attempted to do so, they might have begun to realise that there are difficulties in principle about offering such explanations, more especially if it is thought that quite precise matching (in senses to be defined) might be achieved.

BENNETT AND DESFORGES ON MATCHING

My earlier paper (Davis, 1993) turned first to Bennett, Desforges *et al.* (1984) for an account. They appreciated that interpretations of 'matching' were going to depend on the character of the learning which teachers actually intended for their pupils at particular times. Sometimes a lesson aimed to offer fresh content or new knowledge. On other occasions it would be considered more appropriate to enrich, practise or revise knowledge already possessed. The question whether, for example, a period of teacher exposition or a pupil task directly set by the teacher 'matched' pupil knowledge would have to be interpreted differently depending on the precise intention of the lesson. In short, 'matching' could cover a number of significantly different relationships between current pupil attainment and the teaching or tasks to be presented.

I now turn to a critique of some senses of 'matching' which would seem to have the strongest claim for attention in the educational context. While these senses are loosely based on Bennett and Desforges (1984), they go beyond them. This section aims to be an advance on my earlier paper on matching (Davis, 1993) in that it seeks to create what should be more sophisticated characterizations of matching than those discussed in that article. These stronger candidates are still in the end found wanting.

Matching (1)

The teaching or task is intended to provide the pupils with new knowledge. To decide on how well it is matched, the following two questions must be answered:

(a) To what extent is the knowledge being offered really 'new'?
(b) How far is the new knowledge in comparison with existing knowledge at an appropriate level of difficulty to facilitate its ready acquisition?

If a judgement about matching is made in this first sense, it assumes that pupils' current knowledge, understanding and skills may effectively be assessed. We cannot measure what is new unless we know what is already there before the new is assimilated. Judgements about matching on this interpretation also require that the acquisition of *new* knowledge may be discovered with at least some semblance of accuracy.

Now we evidently can in general terms reach sensible conclusions about what pupils know, understand and can do, and further we are entitled to make judgements about the extent to which they have learned new material. We refrain from introducing Andrea to calculus, given our clear impression that she is not reliable in the ways in which she deals with numbers up to 20. Here we have made a rough judgement about her present attainment. John at the end of

Year 10 seems to have a reasonably impressive grasp of basic electronics, whereas at the end of Year 8, before he began his GCSE electronics course, he knew virtually nothing about the subject. In this second example, we have made a confident appraisal both of John's knowledge in Year 8, and also about the new knowledge he has acquired in two years.

In both examples, the assessments are broad. They make no attempt to go into any detail about specific knowledge, concepts and skills. To do so would be quite unnecessary. The observations may well be sensible and accurate as far as they are intended to go.

The kind of formative assessment which is supposed to facilitate matching does not, of course, resemble these examples at all closely. The data, and the judgements which stem from them, are customarily far more fine-grained and short term. Judgements about matching are being made, not in respect of whole courses, but in respect of particular tasks. I contend that it is at this level that judgements about both someone's current knowledge and new knowledge become elusive and problematic.

The difficulties are easily shown, whether current and new knowledge is thought of as 'declarative', or as 'know-how'. As I observed earlier, many key attainments in education turn out to be complex hybrids of the two. For convenience only, I discuss them in turn here.

MATCHING (1) FOR THE ACQUISITION OF NEW DECLARATIVE KNOWLEDGE

It would be convenient for judgements about matching in the first sense if learning could be viewed as the acquisition of new facts. Then all that would be required is that we could assess which facts are already known by pupils, and detect the new facts acquired after the lesson. Such a view of learning has had few followers in recent decades. Many philosophers, psychologists and educationists have poured scorn on the associated hackneyed imagery portraying minds as 'receptacles' containing facts, to which 'new' facts can be added, perhaps one by one! They have derided the picture of facts in the mind as mental sediments, deposited over periods of time, successively overlain with later material.

Despite the fact that this vision is discredited, it is worthwhile pointing out why it should be rejected in terms of the philosophical considerations developed earlier, since its problems also serve to undermine the first sense of matching given above. In summary, the picture ignores the insights of holism. It was argued earlier that people cannot hold stand-alone, atomistic beliefs, at least if they have a measure of understanding of what they believe, and especially if they are to be able to offer justification which does not involve much deference to the expertise of others. Yet the possibility of precision about new knowledge would appear to rest on the possibility of single beliefs.

Now when a new 'fact' becomes known, connections are established with other material already known. The new transforms the old, and is itself transformed. There is no sense in which the new is separately identifiable. Most will recognise this familiar point as associated with a cluster of views about learning referred to as constructivism, though that term covers a multitude of sins. There are strong echoes here of the classic Piagetian doctrines of assimilation and accommodation. Assimilation is, roughly speaking, making 'new' knowledge fit into existing ways of thinking, concepts, or structures. At the same time, the child's existing ways of thinking, concepts or structures have to be modified to cope with the fresh knowledge. This idea is of course covered by the notion of accommodation. Constructivism comes in when we think of new knowledge having at least in part to be constructed from old. Part of what it is to know something new is to construct appropriate connections with old knowledge. We may be tempted briefly to imagine that it is possible to identify that new 'something' with which connections to the old must be constructed if the new is to be learned. On closer scrutiny, this temptation readily disappears.

A geographical example (cf. Davis, 1993) will illustrate the point. Jane and John listen to some exposition from the teacher, and hear her say 'Edinburgh is west of Bristol'. Jane, we will suppose, was brought up in Edinburgh, and is also well-versed in geography. John has just about heard of each city, and is rather shaky on his compass directions. The teacher is intending to provide the pupils with new knowledge, and so the question arises as to how well her material matches pupils' current knowledge. It is not clear whether pupil ignorance of the relevant fact could be established prior to the lesson. Be that as it may, it is obvious that no coherent meaning can be given to the claim that each pupil has received the *same* thing as a result of the teacher's presentation even if we assume that they both learn something. The impact made on Jane's existing belief network will differ substantially from that made on John's. Jane's knowing that Edinburgh is west of Bristol may have little in common with John's. The words are the same. We will find it very natural to say that they both know the same thing. On closer examination, however, it is difficult to see what is the same about both of them. The idea that each pupil has received the same new, discrete item of information is quite simply untenable.

A further problem with this whole way of thinking of learning is that 'facts' are no more subject to clear identity criteria than are propositions or properties, an issue discussed in the holism chapter. We can only refer to facts using sentences. We may be confident that 'The Prime Minister is boring' would in normal utterance conditions refer to a different fact from 'The universe is expanding'. However we are less sure whether 'Scotland's capital city is west of Bristol' involves a different fact from 'Edinburgh is west of Bristol'. Probably 'Bristol is east of Edinburgh' is different. Yet are we sure? Why is it different, if it is? Perhaps these questions do not admit of definitive answers; it might even be argued that it would be justified to provide different responses depending on what else is known by the contemplator of the 'fact' in question. If Jane and John each *had* learned the same thing from the geography lesson, it would not be possible to identify this precisely. Certainly we can readily use the sentence 'Edinburgh is west of Bristol', and claim that this denotes the fact that both pupils have learned. This natural way of speaking does not, however, despite appearances, enable us to identify clearly and precisely a discrete piece of information which they both acquire from the geography teacher.

It also follows from the adoption of a holist perspective on belief that it is not possible in principle to be exact about what someone knows at any particular time. If the contents of a pupil's mind could be identified with a stock of identifiable discrete beliefs which could be detected by means of some kind of sophisticated assessment device, then this obstacle would not exist. However, it has been argued first that beliefs are not discrete in this way, and secondly that believing something cannot be identified firmly with being in a particular state. Attributions of belief are interpretations, making assumptions about the agent's other beliefs, attitudes, desires and actions. They involve approximate appraisals of a whole cluster of beliefs. These interpretations cannot succeed in characterising definitively and accurately that someone holds a specifiable discrete belief.

To adapt a well-known remark of Wittgenstein (1958, p. 217), if God could look into our minds there would be nothing there for him to see, in virtue of which it would be unambiguously clear that we either believed a given proposition, or failed to believe it.

Fine-grained judgements about both current and new knowledge, then, are impossible if attempts to make the judgements are characterised in terms of questions about resident facts and new facts. Given such a characterisation, it follows from the foregoing argument that judgements about the quality of match between teaching and pupil attainment are not possible in any kind of fine-grained fashion.

MATCHING (1) FOR THE ACQUISITION OF NEW ABILITIES OR SKILLS

We could try to understand the first sense of matching in a different way, moving away from ideas about resident facts and new facts, and thinking instead of *resident abilities and skills*, and the development of *new abilities and skills*. The argument of the previous chapter has established that the whole idea of transfer and traits resists precise conceptualisation. Hence matching judgements dependent upon close assessment of abilities will be defective in principle.

Capacities, abilities and skills in the classroom context purport to be rich traits. They are thought of as manifestable in a great variety of ways. A child would not be credited, for instance, with an 'adding ability' merely because she could put out groups of counters as required, count them up and correctly identify the total. She would also be expected to add with her fingers, to add groups of children as well as of counters, to add without any apparatus, to grasp comparison situations showing 12 as being 3 more than 9, use a number line to complete sentences such as '3 count on 9 is', and so forth. Even a child's incorrect responses might be thought to manifest her ability. Perhaps the child wants to stay with her best friend in a particular group, and not gain promotion which might result from revealing too much mathematical competence. There appear to be few limits on the kinds of behaviour that could, with suitably imagined contexts, count as manifesting 'adding ability'.

While traits of the above kind are envisaged in educational contexts, it turns out that they cannot really exist in the fashion apparently assumed in typical educational discourse. It is not possible to give an account of what counts as already possessing a particular ability, nor of what counts as acquiring a new one. To repeat, this point applies at, so to speak, the microscopic level. Broad, sweeping statements such as 'She has gained many writing competencies which she lacked when she began school three years' are perfectly acceptable as summaries. These are not intended to be precise, and it is not necessary that they should be.

FORMATIVE ASSESSMENT, MATCHING AND ASSUMPTIONS OF LINEARITY

In this section, we discuss question (b) (above, p. 108), an answer to which was required to make judgements about matching for new knowledge or skills. How far is the new knowledge in comparison with existing knowledge at an appropriate level of difficulty to facilitate its ready acquisition?

Plenty of work needs to be done here by the phrase 'at an appropriate level of difficulty'. Earlier we referred to the ways in which 'new' knowledge has to be absorbed into 'old'. At least part of the putative function of formative assessment is the discovery of current attainment, because this is relevant to what *kind* of new material should be offered. It is not simply a matter of knowing what is in fact new for a pupil in comparison with what they already have, but also of obtaining information which helps choices to be made about *suitable* new material. Some may find echoes here of the idea of 'readiness', sometimes attributed to Piaget.

In mathematics, following this thinking through may seem relatively straightforward. It is plausible to claim that learning the subject is sequential. I must learn A before I can learn B, and B before C. I must learn my numbers to 10 before I can learn multiplication. I must learn multiplication before I can learn long division. The issue in connection with assessment and matching will not simply be the appropriateness of the sequencing, but also the size of the 'gap' between A and B, or B and C. If the gap is too great, the children will fail to grasp the new material. If it is too small, it may seem that they are really still 'practising' what they already know. If they have already had plenty of opportunity for practising, this may be time-wasting and provoke boredom.

In English, the subject seems less 'linear'. Nevertheless, in some aspects, an obvious order in which issues should be taught may seem to suggest itself. Apparently I must learn to punctuate with capital letters and full stops before I move on to punctuating dialogue. Or again, I need to understand what sentences are, and to punctuate accordingly, before I can begin to learn to vary the beginnings of my sentences.

In the light of holist insights, I would argue that we should be deeply suspicious of claims for linearity, even in apparently hierarchical subjects. The network of concepts which must be acquired is complex, and its acquisition varies from person to person. We have already seen that it makes little sense to speak either of the acquisition in any definitive fashion of a specific concept or knowledge item, or of the accurate detection of such acquisition. In so far as we can make any sense of broader judgements about children taking in new material, they will not all assimilate it in the same order. Interestingly, empirical studies even in mathematics, such as Denvir and Brown's classic investigation (1986), reflect this point. Jerome Bruner's spiral curriculum ideas have for many years challenged linear conceptions of learning.

Issues relating to the order in which content should be learned have been discussed in some depth by philosophers of education, though much of this was done several decades ago (Hamlyn, 1967; Hirst,

1967). Robert Dearden (1968) spoke of what he called *the fallacy of perfected steps*. He asked 'Does the logical structure of the understanding to be cultivated determine the order in time in which things are to be learned? Are there any necessary temporal priorities here?' (p. 121). To answer in the affirmative is in his view to commit the fallacy of supposing 'that one thing must be perfectly, and not just partially, understood before one can move on to the logically next thing' (p. 121). This point is well made, but it fails to contest the notion of 'logical structure' itself. In Newtonian mechanics, force is connected to mass and acceleration. Is any one of these three key ideas logically fundamental, or prior to the others? Can this question be given a clear sense?

If I think that arithmetic can be generated from set theory, then I might mistakenly think that it followed from this that children should learn set theory first. (The confusion of logical priority with temporal priority in the learning sequence was a favourite theme in 1960s and 1970s philosophy of education.) A deeper mistake still might be to assume that there is some absolute sense in which set theory is *logically prior* to arithmetic. There is no such absolute sense. It is not settled in some Platonic universe which propositions must be treated as axioms, from which the rest of the system may be generated and which in that sense would be regarded as 'logically prior'. Sometimes alternative sets of axioms may be used to generate the same set of theorems. It is not even clear that axioms have to be used at all in the development of formal systems, as witnessed by so-called 'natural deduction' methods in logic (Haack, 1978).

To sum up the difficulty, even if logical structure was thought to entail the desirability of a given learning sequence, it may be doubted whether any incontestable sense of logical priority can be established.

Even if this were not the case, there are plenty of subjects whose so-called logical structure would fail in many educational contexts to provide any hint of proper learning sequences. Suppose my pupils to have completed a module on South Africa. What could I profitably know about any of their individual *geographical* attainments which would make a difference to whether and in what way I start on Australia today? How far could or should their knowledge of electricity make a difference to the level and quality of my teaching about forces today?

Some would argue that the issue here would not be their mastery of specific content. Rather it would be their grasp of more general skills or concepts. In science and geography these might include the notion of the 'fair test', observation skills and capacities to form sensible hypotheses and frame effective means of testing them. I suggest that this move only seems plausible until the concerns about transfer rehearsed in the previous chapter are properly considered.

A different way of conceptualising difficulty levels might be to think about the levels of abstraction exhibited by particular subject matters, and how much more abstract new material is than material successfully absorbed in the recent past. Philosophers of education also turned their attention to this issue. Hamlyn (1978) is a well-known treatment.

This approach could not help to buttress the notion of matching in any comprehensive way, since there are plenty of potential learning sequences which simply do not and should not involve proceeding from the less abstract to the more abstract. Further, it is not true of logical necessity that pupils will find the less abstract 'easier' than the more abstract, and hence that the former should be tackled before the latter. Finally, the very idea of 'abstract' seems to cover a number of significantly different concepts. These seem to include generality, thinking which is relatively independent of experience and discourse in which abstract rather than concrete nouns are mentioned. The three interpretations mentioned are not bound together logically.

Again, it might be argued that the difficulty level of teaching material correlates with its level of complexity. If difficulty levels can be ascertained by assessing complexity levels, then to that extent we can support the possibility of judging how well a task is matched to pupils. Unfortunately, as with the suggestion about levels of abstraction, even if this suggestion could prove helpful in some cases, it cannot do so across the board. Many perfectly legitimate and well thought-out learning sequences simply do not involve proceeding from the less complex to the more, even if other sequences do take pupils in the direction of the more complex. To produce acceptable criteria of 'complexity' might prove to be an intractable problem. Nor is it necessarily the case that all pupils would find the more complex, as defined according to criteria which might prove acceptable to reasonable teachers, more difficult. It will often be the case that within a particular topic the less complex ideas should be introduced first, but arguably there are exceptions, both as regards particular content areas and as regards the impact made on individual pupils.

To conclude our discussion of the first sense of matching, let us sum up the difficulties, and make some positive observations on what actually should happen. Selection of teaching material cannot rest upon any *precise* knowledge of a pupil's current possession of knowledge, understanding and skills. Evidently a broad knowledge of the attainment level of the group to be taught can play a broad-brush role in informing choice of the general level of the teaching to be offered over a substantial period of time. Formative assessment for fine-grained matching in the first sense has no proper function.

'Good' teachers treat pupils differently; they appreciate that pupils vary, sometimes wildly, from one to another in respect of the routes they 'should' follow through the curriculum (Davis, 1993). Some children 'need' to proceed logically and systematically through levels which adults would judge to be of increasing 'difficulty'; other pupils typically proceed 'messily', sometimes jumping to much more 'difficult' levels, and then 'filling in' on later occasions. Some need much practice, others scarcely any; some need much practice at skills of this kind, but hardly any at skills of that kind. Some can 'apply' knowledge and understanding gained in only one or two 'kinds' of context almost immediately to a huge variety of contexts, while others apparently have to be taken through each and every 'new' application, and find it very difficult to 'generalise'.

Matching (2)

The teacher intends pupils to apply in new contexts knowledge or abilities already possessed. To decide on how well the teaching is matched to pupils' current attainments, we ask:

(a) Has the teacher correctly identified the resident knowledge or competence which the lesson seeks to extend?

(b) Does the teaching actually provide the pupils with an opportunity to extend that knowledge or competence?

Bennett *et al.* discuss the idea of 'matching for enrichment', which is close to this second sense of matching. They suggest that a pupil who knows how to multiply might not necessarily realise that multiplication is the operation required in a particular practical context, e.g. putting together equal lengths of ribbon. Hence a suitably matched task would enable the pupil to come to see that multiplication is the operation required in this 'unfamiliar context'.

There are a number of problems here. The most obvious one, in the light of argument already developed, is the difficulty in grasping what is supposed to count as 'knowing how to multiply'. A pupil might possess an algorithmic mechanical skill, enabling her to write or utter correct answers to formal multiplication questions. And of course she might in various ways know and understand rather more than this. A whole range of possible levels of 'connectedness' with other mathematical concepts is possible. She might make links with addition or with division. She might understand what happens when we multiply by 1, or 0, or fractions.

Consider the issue of whether she can use and apply her multiplication capacity at all, or whether it is being envisaged that she only possesses some competence 'in the abstract' or regardless of contexts. In discussions of 'using and applying' in Chapter 2 we explored the possibility that someone can use and apply a piece of mathematics to other areas of mathematics, yet be unable to relate it satisfactorily to the real world. Now suppose our pupil can apply her knowledge to the real world. Again in Chapter 2 we came to appreciate that this in turn could cover several importantly different achievements. Some are so different from others that we cannot link them intelligibly to a purported multiplication ability which may be detected as persisting over a period of time.

As a matter of empirical fact, a pupil in the early stages of multiplication would be unlikely merely to possess an algorithmic skill. Certainly teachers would on the whole prefer not to teach such a skill first, and then proceed to help pupils apply it in various ways, though admittedly some children seem to sequence their learning in this way.

It would be relatively easy to assess whether a pupil has a thin algorithmic skill. It is much more difficult to pinpoint how much more she might possess besides this thin competence. The supposed multiplication competence as described lacks a clear identity. The idea that teaching *might extend a particular competence* rests on a mythological notion of traits. My argument suggests that nothing can be done about this. The associated matching judgements cannot be precise or rigorous.

Ideas of 'extending' existing contexts, or of 'new' contexts, may themselves depend upon notions of similarity to which we have paid so much destructive attention in earlier discussion. We certainly cannot help ourselves to any kind of unproblematic notion of *context type* which would help us to explicate matching in this sense.

Matching (3)

The teacher intends pupils to practise skills already possessed. The judgement about matching must ask:

(a) Has the teacher correctly identified pupils' possession of skill A?
(b) Does the teaching enable pupils to practise skill A?

Matching (4)

The teacher intends pupils to recall and practise knowledge and skills already possessed but which have not been recently exercised. The judgement about matching must ask:

(a) Has the teacher correctly judged that pupils did possess given knowledge or skill at any time in the past?

(b) Does the teaching enable pupils to recall the relevant knowledge or skill and to practise it?

Both these notions of matching seem rather more defensible than the first two. Nevertheless, unless the skills are explicitly algorithmic or observably physical, there are going to be the now familiar problems about what counts as possessing a particular skill. Equally, what counts as practising or recalling that 'same' skill or area of knowledge is an issue which cannot be settled definitively.

The upshot of these reflections is this. An alleged major function of assessment, namely formative assessment to aid matching, often cannot in principle produce results in the detailed form which would be required to support decisions about the type and level of teaching to offer pupils. The word 'often' is there, leaving open the possibility that in *some* subject areas more plausibly construed as collections of specifiable skills (e.g. physical education) formative assessment might still retain a legitimate role. Formative assessment falters most significantly where cognitive abilities and any kind of 'rich' declarative knowledge is concerned.

Perhaps, then, teachers' failure to place formative assessment at the heart of teaching not only springs from formidable logistical difficulties, but from an intuitive sense that there is something unreal about the whole project. I refer here to attempts to assess specific cognitive achievement. At the end of the book I will look briefly at other personal qualities which might be assessed with a view to enhancing the teaching process.

IMPLICATIONS FOR THE ORGANISATION OF LEARNING

In the first chapter, it was observed that the style of curriculum planning known as *differentiation by task* was or should be associated with a strong emphasis on formative assessment, with its purported potential for the accurate pinpointing of pupils' current attainment. Teachers particularly in the primary sector have been criticised over the years for their failure to provide adequate 'differentiation', as the quotations from government documents at the start of this chapter suggest. More recently, the pendulum has swung in the opposite direction. Now, it almost seems that teachers, especially in the UK, are criticised for *creating* differences between pupils by their practice of 'differentiation'.

> The (Cockcroft) Committee drew attention to the *wide variation in pupils'*
> *attainments*: . . . the subsequently famous 'seven year difference' in attainments
> . . . it did not seem to have crossed the Committee's mind that the variability of

pupils' attainments in other countries might be lower, perhaps as a result of different methods of teaching or the different organisation of curricula (Prais, 1995).

Recently some commentators have cast envious looks at the educational practices of 'successful' Pacific Rim economies such as Taiwan. A particular focus has been their seemingly effective and stimulating whole-class teaching methods. It is not entirely clear that such whole-class teaching methods are being favoured for *educational reasons*, since it must be obvious to these commentators that there are plenty of singularly unsuccessful economies where whole-class teaching methods also predominate. Be that as it may, it cannot be denied that the arguments developed in this chapter in effect encourage new thinking about the potential of whole-class teaching. In the UK these implications are especially significant for the primary sector. Whole-class teaching of various kinds has always been offered in primary schools, and this continues. Yet there is certainly a strong perception that it plays a less significant role than it should, and that it assumed a particularly low profile in 'child-centred' primary schools in the 1960s and 1970s. (In secondary schools these kinds of perceptions and political forces are less prominent. Direct teaching has often been to class-sized groups. Individualised schemes of work have also been influential, especially in mathematics. In subjects such as technology the very nature of the activities normally pursued has entailed small group work.)

In the primary sector two styles of organising learning are sometimes chosen in place of whole-class teaching. The first consists of individualised work programmes, which have been prominent particularly in mathematics. The second is the division of pupils into four or five attainment groups, and the provision of distinctive teaching for each group. The latter has been marketed as a powerful strategy for appropriate differentiation, especially in the core subjects.

The arguments in this book serve to cast doubt on one set of considerations which are normally thought to favour these alternatives to whole-class teaching. If formative assessment cannot in principle deliver detailed information about pupils' cognitive attainment then a traditionally important argument for teaching individuals, or pupils grouped by attainment, is shown to be weak.

My conclusions must not be overstated, however. *Fine-grained* assessment may well not be necessary for the teacher to note that such and such a group produce several paragraphs when engaged in 'free writing' while others scarcely string three words together. Such facts about a particular class might still suggest the desirability of teaching by attainment groups from time to time.

Note that there are reasons for valuing teaching styles other than whole-class teaching which have no clear link with the availability of information about individual pupils' cognitive achievements. These reasons include the necessity to motivate pupils, and to take proper account of whether they can concentrate in one particular learning mode for more than a certain length of time. (Other *objections* to group or individual teaching methods have also been canvassed, such as that group work is very difficult to organise, or that individual work is socially isolating and extremely inefficient in terms of the use of teacher time. This is not the place to review these arguments; they are very important, but practical or empirical in character.)

There is a sense in which differentiation by task represents teachers' aspirations to a formidable degree of control over the level and quality of pupil learning. The difficulties about detailed formative assessment undermine teachers' capacities to operate a differentiation by task approach effectively. Indeed, such difficulties might be thought to open the door once more to arguments that pupils could, and possibly should, be afforded more control over their own learning.

Now a move to more whole-class teaching, and a transfer of control over learning from teacher to pupils, do not at first sight go together. Indeed the two are usually associated with sharply differing political perspectives. Incidentally it is interesting that those favouring whole-class teaching are also likely to advocate as much setting in the secondary school as possible, and even selective schooling. Perhaps on reflection we can understand that these positions may be held together without inconsistency, given that fine-grained assessment is not required to determine the members of the top maths set or entrants to the local grammar school.

The apparent tension between whole-class teaching and pupils exercising control over their learning arguably springs from a failure to appreciate the range of styles which whole-class teaching might encompass. If we accept that we cannot pinpoint individual pupils' knowledge, we are not thereby overturning the conventional wisdom that there is a huge range within any one class-sized teaching group, and that this is the case even where the children have been carefully allocated to sets according to their attainment. A different orthodoxy is under attack. We are relinquishing the dream that we the teachers can have a god's eye view of pupil knowledge and can teach 'accordingly'.

Teaching styles still need to take account of the fact that there will be a range within a class, a range of attitudes, maturities, concentration, of ability in the loosest, most colloquial sense and that some pupils will know a good deal more than others. How this should be done is not the province of the philosopher. Brief indication can be given of approaches which at least seem compatible with scepticism about fine-grained matching. How can whole-class teaching be blended with pupils having a greater degree of control over their own learning?

Possibilities include the use of interactive questioning styles which allow pupils to respond at their own level. In whole-class contexts pupils could be encouraged to take more initiatives about the direction of the lesson and the approach to be adopted for the task. Approaches to whole-class teaching which continue to be ruled out include the extraordinary lesson 'scripts', referred to in Chapter 1, produced by Jennings and Dunne (1997). It is a measure of their consistency, if not of the value of their educational approach, that these writers defend a different kind of knowledge and understanding from that developed in this book. They do not see new knowledge as necessarily having to 'connect' with resident knowledge and understanding. Pupils in their view can be given abstract knowledge which they then can learn to 'apply'. In the light of the holist considerations developed earlier, together with the treatment of rule following, we are unlikely to understand very readily how there can be such cognitive achievement as the abstract knowledge they seek to conjure with.

It may also be argued that far more use should be made of *differentiation by outcome* than is currently the case. Such a suggestion cannot be properly explained without conceding that the familiar distinction between differentiation *by task* and by *outcome* is not philosophically tight. For instance, asking a whole class of young children to write a story would normally be cited as an example of teaching involving differentiation by outcome. Let us unpack this illustration a little even though in practice the teacher would be unlikely to set up the lesson so baldly.

The 'same' task is apparently set to all pupils. Their responses will be in a great range of shapes, sizes and qualities. However, to the extent that the teacher will have different expectations of different pupils from the outset, and that this fact is well-understood by the pupils, the differentiation prevailing in the lesson does not await the 'outcome', namely pupils' finished products. Pupils thought to be 'able' by the teacher, who know this, understand that they are not being set the same task as others perceived as 'slow learners'. The former will be quite clear that three or four sentences, with a lack of attention to spelling and punctuation, will simply not be acceptable. They are being asked to write several pages and to exercise their imaginations impressively, even if this is not made explicit in this particular lesson. Equally, other pupils will know that the production of a few sentences, with attempts at basic literacy, will earn praise from the teacher. Even though the teacher may contend that she is setting the same task to all the pupils, this is not actually the case.

In practice, as I said, matters mostly would proceed less crudely than this, and the teacher may give varying follow-up instructions to different pupils which modify the common task of story writing. *Prima facie* differentiation by outcome is in practice heavily coloured by constraints from the teacher which have more than a whiff of differentiation by task.

In suggesting more use of differentiation by outcome, then, I am arguing that teachers should at least sometimes offer classes the same task in such a way that the pupils can exercise choice over the quality of their responses. The old concerns about self-fulfilling prophecies tend to the same recommendation. If teachers come to appreciate fully the principled limitations of their access to their pupils' 'current knowledge', they will sometimes offer teaching where pupils genuinely have scope to respond at a level and in a fashion which is not constrained or predicted in advance by the teacher. Perhaps pupils sometimes have a little more insight than teachers into the complex psychological states which underlie their performances. For some of the time at least, tasks must be 'open', where pupils make choices about how to proceed, and even on occasion in what direction to proceed. While sometimes specific solutions or answers may be required, there are strong arguments that teachers should not *always* make demands of this kind.

Whole-class teaching styles incorporating this thinking cannot be restricted to the teacher working interactively with all the children at once, even if this is a significant element. Lessons might well include periods during which smaller groups of pupils focus on problems and discuss them. The results can be shared later with the class as a whole.

The argument in this chapter would also suggest a measure of caution in respect of the custom of tiered entry to GCSEs, with some pupils judged incapable of scoring the highest grades and so entered at a lower level. However, the practice may not be definitively ruled out, since fine-grained judgements about pupil achievement do not seem to be required for its continuance. I have little hope that this practice will cease, even though there are known to be practical difficulties associated with it.

Early in the history of the National Curriculum it appeared that primary teachers were being asked to keep very extensive assessment records on children. Reference was made in the first chapter to the way in which the National Curriculum assessment structure attempted to combine two distinct assessment aims, the formative and the summative. It is difficult to say how clearly teachers made this distinction, or indeed whether they saw much practical use for the evidence they were accumulating. Given the detail that was thought to be required, it has to be assumed that at least part of the purpose was formative, and to assist better matching. The information was of the wrong kind to feed into summative assessment reports, and would scarcely be digestible by those demanding that schools should account for their performance through assessment results.

For practical reasons, much less evidence is now being stored. To the extent that it was being kept to aid matching, my suggestion would be that very much less still should be retained. Information about what pupils have 'covered', and a broad comment on attitude and 'aptitude', is compatible with what we understand about the nature of learning and knowledge and our inherent capacities to detect its presence.

In the next chapter, we look in more depth at the language in which information from formative assessment for accountability purposes would need to be couched. New problems are encountered in the context of a philosophical examination of some key ideas associated with assessment, namely reliability and validity.

Chapter 8
Reliability, Validity and
Criterion-referencing

Chapter 1 discussed the move away from norm- to criterion-referencing in assessment. This shift has occurred both in public examinations and standardised tests, and in the character of more informal teacher judgements. Emphasis on criterion-referencing seems to fit quite naturally with contemporary thinking about so-called 'authentic' and practical assessment of what pupils 'actually' know, understand and can do. The concern is no longer with an abstract grade reflecting how a pupil fares in relation to her peers, but with 'information' about her real capabilities.

The National Curriculum for England and Wales, and also various Graded Assessment Schemes, provide 'official' descriptions of pupil achievement. Pupils transfer from class to class or from school to school and reports on their attainments are supplied. In theory teachers across the nation should share an understanding and interpretation of the common language in which these reports are expressed. Both SATs and Teacher Assessment within the National Curriculum are supposed to provide results within this shared conception of achievement. Schools are said to vary widely in their capacity to ensure that pupils acquire given levels of knowledge and understanding. The assumption is that what it is for a pupil to possess such and such knowledge and understanding, characterised in National Curriculum language, is the 'same', whatever class or school they attend. On this basis, schools can be held to account for their success or failure in promoting learning defined in these standard ways.

In the UK the Teacher Training Agency has drawn up lists of competencies which student teachers must acquire by the time they are credited with Newly Qualified Teacher status. The profiles in which these competencies are reported are to be carried forward by the students into their careers as teachers. This implies that, for instance, the claim that a student 'presents subject content accurately, coherently and clearly in ways which stimulate, motivate and enthuse pupils' should mean the same whether reported of a student by Durham University, Exeter University, a representative of a School Centred Initial Teacher Training Course or OFSTED. Initial Teacher Training institutions are now to be held to account for whether beginning teachers are in possession of all these competencies or 'Standards'. The language in which the 'Standards' are characterised purports to identify with precision a range of specific capacities appropriate for beginning teachers.

In this chapter I want to focus initially on the role of National Curriculum attainment descriptions in the kind of accountability exercise outlined above, and on the ways in which teacher assessment and the results of SATs relate to the meaning of the descriptions. I argue that if these knowledge, understanding and skill descriptions are to incorporate appropriate 'proper' or 'rich' elements then they cannot in principle possess the national currency envisaged for them. In the course of the argument, an examination is made of ideas about validity and reliability, as they are applied in contemporary educational assessment contexts. The fruits of the discussion are then applied to competency-based assessment of teachers in training.

It has become received wisdom among assessment professionals that it is very difficult if not impossible to achieve assessment results which are both reliable and valid at one and the same time. For instance, Cohen and Manion (1989) discuss the example of interviewing. 'Where increased reliability of the interview is brought about by greater control of its elements, this is achieved . . . at the cost of reduced validity' (p. 318). Empirical reasons for this may be suggested. The interviewer may seek to be detached and controlling in order that her treatment of one interviewee is comparable to her treatment of another. Yet such an approach may inhibit the interviewee from expressing what she really thinks and feels. Thus the interview process is less 'valid' than it would have been had the interviewer been more natural and relaxed.

However the 'difficulty' about combining validity and reliability is arguably a point of principle, rather than a temporary obstacle which advances in assessment expertise would eventually overcome (see Davis, 1995). I contended that it *is* in fact possible to achieve high degrees of reliability and validity but only in respect of some assessment procedures employed to probe very 'narrow' kinds of achievement. I have defended these points further (Davis, 1996a) against criticism (Winch and Gingell, 1996).

Moreover, in the light of the general critique of assessment mounted in Chapter 5, we can appreciate the principled objections to the kind of assessment of rich or proper knowledge and skill which aspires to precision and comprehensiveness. In short, Chapter 5 began to develop claims that much assessment of rich knowledge cannot be valid.

While the concepts of reliability and validity were originally 'technical', and developed in the contexts of psychometric tests, there have been attempts at a radical extension of these ideas. The objective has been to enable them to be applied to practical and 'authentic' forms of assessment. Within these procedures pupils are assessed in respect of behaviour and performance of a kind which is actually thought valuable. Their performance is judged in real or realistic contexts, rather than ratings being made of their responses to tests out of context (Linn *et al.*, 1991; Moss, 1992; Messick, 1994).

THE COMMON LANGUAGE: OBTAINING RELIABILITY AT THE EXPENSE OF VALIDITY

It is important to examine the relationship between the requirement for a standardised meaning for pupil attainment descriptions, and the kind of reliability in principle obtainable from the assessments employed to justify the attainment descriptions' applications. We need to probe more deeply into conceptions of reliability to elaborate on this line of thought any further.

One conception of test reliability involves asking whether pupils would perform at the same level if the test is administered on more than one occasion. This itself is ambiguous. It might refer to whether pupils would actually be awarded the same score by a given marker on different occasions *on the assumption that they actually produce the same answers*. Or it might refer to whether pupils produce consistent performances from one administration of the test to another.

Another version of reliability is linked to whether the pupil would receive the same score even if a particular set of test responses were assessed by different markers. If the 'test' consists of a set essay, for instance, it will not be reliable in either sense (Williams, 1992, p. 56).

In some kinds of test, reliability as characterised above could not be measured in practice. If someone has already taken a particular test, then even after the lapse of a year or so they are very likely to carry memories of the earlier attempt. For this reason if not for others the chances of the response to a later administration of the test being at least similar to the earlier would appear reasonably high. The degree of correspondence between the scores need owe little to the 'reliability' of the test itself. Perhaps only a chance blow to the head just after the first attempt, causing the candidate to lose all memories of the test, would enable reliability in this sense to be checked.

Conventionally, one way round this problem is splitting the test into halves, and giving one half on the first occasion with the other half on the second occasion. (Obviously this would be impossible with certain sorts of tasks, such as the essay question referred to above.) Alternatively another version of the 'same' test is constructed using item banks of some kind.

These manoeuvres involve the difficulty referred to in Chapter 6, that a preconceived notion of 'item type' may have to be deployed. The split-half reliability method depends on the idea that each half of the test is assessing the 'same' knowledge, process or skills. Item banks need some uncontentiously applicable criterion of 'sameness' to decide which items belong together in a particular category. It has been argued in Chapter 6 that such a criterion is not available in respect of much of the cognitive achievement with which education concerns itself.

My observations so far apply to the reliability of written tests. It is held by a variety of educational assessment professionals that it may be extended to the making of judgements about pupils in practical situations. These might simply be test contexts in which pupils are supposed to show what they know and understand, rather than merely write it. In more informal possibilities, complex individual or group behaviour when working on particular tasks in specified contexts might form the focus of judgements made by teachers or other assessors. Here, two types of reliability might be distinguished (James and Conner, 1993), namely *inter-judge reliability and intra-judge reliability*. The former refers to the degree of agreement between two assessors, while the latter refers to the consistency of an assessor's judgements on different occasions.

The great and obvious advantage of written responses in terms of facilitating reliability judgements is that they are permanent. They can be inspected by a particular assessor on more than one occasion over a period of time. Or they may be scrutinised by more than one assessor. Even in this straightforward case, it would be important that the actual appearance of the answers was kept the same. Some will recall the notorious experiment many years ago in which the same scripts were submitted for an English A-level examination, but with different candidate names and handwriting. The grades awarded varied from 'A' to 'E'.

As soon as we move away from written responses the situation becomes more difficult to analyse. What is it that can be examined by a particular assessor on several occasions, or by more than one assessor? Can a specific performance produced in response to a question or piece of task setting be appropriately scrutinised for reliability? Certainly more than one assessor could view the same performance, and their reactions be compared. Suppose the same assessor's judgements are to be compared over a period of time. Perhaps a video record is made, so that the same act token and context is the object of each judgement.

If on the other hand the assessor were expected to judge that a second act token was an instance of the same type as a previous act token in order that the judgements could be compared, we are entering more difficult territory. Our earlier reflections (above p. 75–105) stimulated by the Situated Cognition tradition should alert us to the potential complexities involved in typing act-tokens.

If the pupil merely has to produce a specific physical performance, e.g. a particular jump on the trampoline, then we may well be perfectly clear what is entailed in judgements of sameness. A physical property of an act is at issue. Its exemplification can be easily identified in a variety of contexts. The latter do not impinge on the salient physical characteristic of the action. Of course, great care would need to be taken to ensure that the pupil was set the task in the 'same kind of way'. For instance, the tone of voice and language used would need to be held constant. Also pupils should have the same kinds of perceptions of the physical and social settings in which they were being asked to produce the jumps.

Where a practical performance is taken as an expression of a cognitive achievement we can no longer make judgements of 'sameness' according to physical characteristics. Consider practical tests, for instance of the kind exploited by the APU. The assessors can be required to work precisely to interview scripts. So, using the standard language laid before them, they can set up specific tasks for pupils.

To take up a theme once more which was raised in Chapter 5, it may be asked at this point how in principle it could be made clear what is to count as a correct answer, or practical response. Imagine that candidates are permitted to produce any one of a variety of ways of expressing a response, or any one of a variety of actions which count as the correct response. We then have the possibility that different interpretations might be made by different assessors, or that the same assessor might not respond consistently to the 'same' response (a physically similar action in a physically similar context). To avoid this opportunity for inconsistency in judgements the designers of the practical tasks would be driven to prescribing very exactly which responses were 'appropriate'. A comprehensive video record might go some way towards making such practical tests as amenable to reliability discourse as written responses. It still may inadvertently omit some crucial features of the context and the pupil response. The close prescription of appropriate responses has serious consequences for the role of rich or proper knowledge. We return to this theme later.

Let us turn now to the criterion-referenced National Curriculum of England and Wales, and by implication similar systems such as some Graded Assessment Schemes. Issues of reliability or consistency arise in several crucial ways. The core subjects have 'level descriptions'. If pupils are judged capable of a sufficient number of the descriptions given at a particular level, they are supposed to be assigned to that level. Alternatively, pupils are assigned levels according to their score in SATs.

Are teachers consistent in their application of level descriptions? This question breaks down into further sub-questions. Would the teacher judge consistently on the basis of given evidence about a particular pupil that they were at such and such a level, if it were possible to provide the teacher with separate opportunities to make the judgement? (Similar practical difficulties arise as in written tests above, since the teacher might well remember their first judgement.) Would different teachers, on the basis of given evidence X, judge a pupil P to be at level *n*? If pupils P and Q are judged to be at the same level by a particular teacher, would they in fact in some relevant sense *have* 'closely similar' achievements? If pupil P is judged to be at level *n* by one teacher, while pupil Q is judged to be at level *n* by a second teacher, would P and Q have 'closely similar' achievements in any sense accepted by the profession at large?

A philosopher is not needed here to provide the obvious answer of 'not necessarily'. The notion of 'best fit' according to which pupils are awarded a particular level by teachers according to the Level Description they fit best is inherently and intentionally imprecise. If 'information' about these levels is not supposed to be comparable between schools, and to possess any kind of national currency, then perhaps none of this matters very much. Of course, some might wonder in that case whether there can be any purpose in assigning pupils to these levels.

Someone broadly in favour of a criterion-referenced set of National Curriculum descriptions might concede at this point that Level Descriptions represent an unfortunate twist of policy. They are inherited from the previous version of the National Curriculum, with its statements of Attainments expressed in ten levels. Level Descriptions could actually be abandoned while retaining the heart of the system: the descriptions of pupil achievement with national currency.

I now argue that putting to one side the problems of Level Descriptions only allows much deeper difficulties to emerge. As this argument develops, it takes us forward into issues of much wider significance than those presented by the current version of the UK National Curriculum.

Level Descriptions are made up of components which purport to be characterisations of pupil knowledge, understanding and skills. Similar language is used in the programmes of study. Consider an extract (following Davis, 1995) from level 5 of Attainment Target 2 'Number and Algebra' from the Mathematics version of the National Curriculum: 'Pupils understand and use an appropriate non-calculator method for solving problems that involve multiplying and dividing any three digit number by any two digit number' (DFE, 1995b).

It is essential, presumably, that there is consistency in the application of this component. As it stands, it appears to lend itself to a variety of construals. It does not specify which method pupils must use, and there are arguably quite a number of non-calculator procedures which would meet the case. Some might be less efficient than others or more long-winded. Certain pupils might find a given method difficult to learn in comparison with another. 'Appropriateness' might be possessed in virtue of one or more of these features. Various criteria for appropriateness may even turn out to conflict with each other. Then there is the use of the term 'problems'. What is supposed to count as a problem? On the face of it this category might include anything from numerical questions written on paper in vertical format, to 'realistic' practical challenges whose solution requires a multiplication or a division to be carried out. Finally 'understand and use' is a phrase the meaning of which we have spent several chapters trying to unravel. In Chapter 2 we saw in particular something of the extent of the range of uses and applications to which knowledge might be put.

How could consistency be ensured? Can the ambiguity of the descriptions of potential pupil attainment be avoided? I intend to develop an argument that the ambiguity cannot be avoided without serious damage to the official or standard language. We are not confronted here with an incompetently devised set of descriptions, the deficiencies of which might be remedied if sufficient time and expertise is devoted to the matter. There have of course been arguments among the professionals about the details of the descriptions, but I have no intention of joining the discussion on this level. My claim is rather that the difficulty is intrinsic to the nature of the whole enterprise. To the extent that ways can be found to remove ambiguity, and hence improve the chances of consistency or reliability, the conceptions of the pupil achievements concerned will be distorted and narrowed in the direction of thin procedures or thin knowledge.

Mere translations of the official attainment descriptions are not going to help. They will be abstract and general to a degree, and equally susceptible of a range of interpretations. The situation here is reminiscent of our earlier investigations into the complexities inherent in the formulation of a rule and the role of the Background in ensuring a consistent application of the rule's verbal formulation. The trouble with descriptions of knowledge and understanding is that we lack a set of Background practices which are sufficiently clearly and universally established to ensure a consistent application of these descriptions. Legislation as enshrined in clauses agreed by parliament has an analogous problem, and requires in England at least the system of precedents to buttress its consistent application.

If abstraction and generality are the 'problem', it may be asked why we do not opt for the obvious solution, and offer examples. Some teachers welcomed the advent of SATs because, in their view, the tasks served to clarify the meaning of the general descriptions of pupil attainment (see Davis, 1995). Other developments on a school or even national scale have paralleled this. SCAA now produces 'Exemplification of Standards' booklets containing examples of pupil work to illustrate particular level descriptions. They issue health warnings about these illustrations with a deceptively disarming reference to the richer knowledge teachers will have of pupils. For instance:

> The material in each profile can only be representative of the range of materials and experiences which contribute to a teacher's knowledge of each child. It cannot replicate the extent of the knowledge that you will have built up about each of your children over time and across a range of situations, and which you will use to make rounded judgements about the levels which best fit your children's performance (SCAA, 1996).

Incidentally teachers experienced in the ways of assessment would be unlikely to be happy with portfolios which merely contained written products. They would expect details included of the context in which the task was set, the language in which it was set, and so forth.

How then might SATs or the contents of portfolios enable official attainment descriptions to be 'clarified' and used consistently? It may be thought that the answer to this question is straightforward. Is it not simply a matter of comparing a current pupil's work, and aspects of the context and task setting, with the SAT activity or with an item in the portfolio? An exact match seems unlikely. The more approximate the match, the less likely it is that the teacher is cashing out the attainment description in the 'same' way as that embodied in the SAT or in the portfolio item. Debates about the contents of portfolios with the object of ensuring a shared understanding of the attainment descriptions would appear to amount to a process in which the descriptions are stripped of their abstraction and generality. Specific exemplar tasks are brought in to fill the void.

However, I would argue that consistency is not so easily obtained as this. As we saw in the discussion of actions and traits in Chapter 6, a pupil performance (an act token) is susceptible of a range of descriptions. It may be thought of as being several different act types. The child joining groups of bricks together is performing physical movements, making a clattering noise, adding two numbers with a total less than twenty, and so forth. The descriptions may incorporate community-held systems of concepts. They may seek to mirror closely how, as it is presumed, the agent thinks of his or her performance. On the other hand, the descriptions may echo the *de re* style of belief reporting, where the speaker who seeks to classify the performance is commenting at least in part on how the performance relates to community-held conventions or concepts, regardless of how it is felt that the agent views his or her performance.

The exemplar will feature in the portfolio as being of a certain type. The characterisation could be very general, or highly specific. It could be abstract, or it could be physical. Although abstract descriptions are often general, they may not be, whereas physical descriptions are more likely to be specific. It would be a mistake, presumably, if the action characterisation did not reflect the way in which it was seen by the agent in question. To make it probable that the action description did mirror the way in which its performer thought of it, more would be needed in the portfolio in addition to the exemplar itself. This should include a good deal of background information about the pupil, other aspects of their performances, contributions in discussions, and so on. (I do not think that portfolios are actually being filled with this kind of information, and teachers would doubtless say that any proposal to do so would be wholly impractical.)

National Curriculum language itself may be used to characterise the exemplars. For example, a given portfolio entry might be credited with being an instance where a pupil can 'carry through substantial tasks and solve quite complex problems by breaking them down into smaller, more manageable tasks' (DFE, 1995b). This is a very broad category, and could obviously cover a vast number of performances which might differ in other respects. Compare this with the description '[Pupils] construct pie charts' (DFE, 1995b). A far narrower category is envisaged here, though if we wished to be awkward we could have an interesting time inventing various possible processes which 'construct' might cover.

Both examples from the National Curriculum may be interpreted variously. If a portfolio entry was said to be an instance of problem-solving, this could not help to secure consistency without further constraints being laid down. If a teacher wishes to compare a performance from a current pupil with the problem-solving exemplar, what common features precisely should be sought? However much discussion there might be between teachers or between schools about problem solving, consistent practice is not going to occur in a system in which teachers are expected simply to refer to portfolio exemplars of it.

How might consistency be improved here? The obvious move would be to narrow down the description of the exemplar, pointing up particular features which another performance must share if it is to count as the 'same', and hence warrant the relevant attainment description taken from the National Curriculum. What kind of 'narrowing down' is going to be effective? Detailed correspondences between the performance at issue and the exemplar, these corres-pondences not being described in abstract terms, would seem to be the answer. Procedural resemblances would have to obtain which took little or no account of the way the performances might be embedded in rich declarative knowledge. In the use of exemplars we seem to be moving away from a 'sensible' interpretation of the relevant attainment statement.

More optimism over the construction of pie charts might be thought justified, since this is a far less general performance characterisation in the first place. The exemplar could incorporate details of precisely what the 'construction' amounted to, the way the task was set, the equipment if any supplied to and used by the pupils and so forth. Now an 'intelligent' approach would apparently be to characterise the exemplar actions and processes so as to permit teachers to decide in a flexible and common-sense way whether any of a variety of pupil performances in classroom contexts 'come to the same thing' or 'involve the same mathematics' as the exemplar pie-chart construction. Yet if this approach were adopted, far too much leeway would be being granted to teachers. Licence for inconsistent decisions about which classroom performances matched the portfolio exemplar would be built in. In order to reduce the likelihood of inconsistency, there would have to be a movement towards thin procedural descriptions of constructing a pie chart, and towards matching the exemplar in crude and probably observably physical respects.

MORE ABOUT VALIDITY

I want now to take the discussion further by making some reference to current ideas about validity. As noted above, although the concept was developed originally in connection with psychometric tests, it is turning up in enhanced and more sophisticated guise in relation to 'authentic' forms of assessment. The notion of 'authentic' is often used in association with the assessment of performances. Teachers enjoined by the National Curriculum to provide their own pupil assessments to supplement SATs results, and who do this on the basis of observing a wealth of pupil performances in a range of contexts, are *prima facie* involved in some kind of 'authentic' assessment.

Messick (1994) discusses the meaning of 'authentic' ('direct' is also used as a synonym). It sometimes appears that any performance provides the opportunity for a more direct or authentic assessment, in comparison with for instance multiple-choice tests or other traditional written examinations. With a little more reflection, it may be said that '. . . authentic assessments aim to capture a richer array of student knowledge and skill than is possible with multiple choice tests; to depict the processes and strategies by which students produce their work; to align the assessment more directly with the ultimate goals of schooling; and to provide realistic contexts for the production of student work by having the tasks and processes . . . parallel those in the real world' (Messick, 1994, p. 18).

This characterisation still fails to pin down the idea of authenticity. Tasks and contents could resemble 'real world' contexts, and be said to be authentic in that sense. Or instead they might faithfully reflect what has been happening in the curriculum and in the classroom. Messick tries to clarify and to distinguish between some of these aspects of authenticity. He suggests that a particular task closely approximating to something in the real world might be said to possess *fidelity*. Or the range of circumstances encountered in 'real' settings might be mirrored to some extent in the assessments. This he characterises as *comprehensiveness*. (Much has already been said about the principled difficulties inherent in the ideas of mirroring or capturing either what happens in the real world, or what has been happening in the school curriculum. At the heart of these difficulties lies the notion of 'resemblance'.)

Evidently such diverse aspirations to authenticity might give rise to conflicting demands on the constructors of tasks. Moreover, in yet another attempt to capture an idea of authenticity, it might be said to characterise *contextualised* as opposed to *decontextualised* tests. We have already in effect discussed the wealth of possible meanings of 'contextualised' in earlier treatment of 'using and applying'. I suggest that enough has already been said to cast doubt on the way 'authentic' is used in some assessment literature. It is supposed to carry a positive evaluation of some kind. Yet it is so imprecise that much analysis is required of a particular use before we can decide whether we support such positive evaluation.

One broad thrust of claims about authentic assessment seems to relate to validity itself. Authentic assessments are said to be the most 'valid' assessments. 'Valid' assessments are thought to capture what they are supposed to measure, namely the actual knowledge and skills which pupils possess. The TGAT Report (DES, 1988) strongly influenced the nature of the original SATs, where the activities required closely resembled ongoing kinds of classroom experiences. One of the justifications for this type of authenticity seemed to be that the SATs would be to that extent more valid. It was not always made explicit that there was an assumed concern to probe proper or rich knowledge, and hence 'valid' in this context meant that the SATs would be better able to measure the presence of rich knowledge.

The ideal of the original SATs has unsurprisingly vanished as being 'impractical', and so it was, given the severe constraints of money and resources under which schools labour. It is still suggested by government agencies (e.g. SCAA, 1996, p.7) that teacher assessment ranks with SATs as of equal importance, and many would imagine that teacher assessment makes up in validity that which is now absent from the SATs.

Since 'validity' is supposed to be a property of tests or other definable assessment tasks, how can this term even be discussed in connection with the more informal teacher assessments required by the National Curriculum? In the case of teacher assessment the exemplar tasks in the portfolios might have to be credited with validity levels. Given the function of these exemplars, the question whether they are valid is the question whether their successful performance is a good indication that pupils possess the knowledge, understanding and skills in the relevant National Curriculum statements.

If the meaning of National Curriculum statements about pupil knowledge and understanding is 'cashed' or clarified by reference to exemplar tasks, it is being distorted. We have seen just how elusive and imprecise notions of 'rich' knowledge and skills can be. Yet this elusiveness does not prevent it being abundantly clear that (repeated?) performance on a strictly limited set of specific tasks cannot constitute such knowledge. In so far as we have any grip on the notion of rich knowledge, it is rather that success on such a task might be a *manifestation* of rich knowledge.

The purported 'clarification' of the meaning of statements about knowledge and understanding through exemplar tasks is in fact no such thing. There has been considerable official backing both for the idea that the kinds of tasks found in SATs tell teachers what attainment descriptions really mean, and for the use of exemplars to the same end. However I do not think that policy-makers really intended that National Curriculum terminology should be subjected to this kind of reduction. It is damaging to teaching and learning in two kinds of ways.

The first may be summed up as the classic danger that teachers will devise methods to elicit the kind of behaviour constituting successful performance on the tasks, rather than methods promoting rich knowledge and understanding. Some observations were made about this in Chapter 5. We are now ready to take the issue a little further.

It is an empirical question whether teachers will succumb to this kind of pressure on their teaching styles, and on the whole in this book I am avoiding empirical questions about pedagogy. Moreover it could be argued that teaching methods efficiently promoting the production of certain kinds of behaviour will not *necessarily* ignore entirely the kind of knowledge and understanding which might profitably underlie the behaviour.

Further, it is true that children's knowledge and understanding must begin somewhere, that understanding develops gradually, and that the kinds of conceptual networks which are appropriate for a rich understanding and to support the possibility of a good range of uses and applications cannot be, so to speak, put into the child's mind all at once. These observations echo remarks made by Winch and Gingell in their critique of Davis (1995), where they took me to be discussing pedagogy:

Suppose, by the end of schooling, we wished our pupils to be able to intelligently and critically analyse poetry. What might we do to further this end and examine whether we have achieved it? We might ... decide ... to separate the elements of critical analysis and teach and test to these elements ... In teaching each part some of what we teach will be concerned with mechanical — or 'thin' — skills ... some of our lessons will be concerned to teach not merely identification of such things but judgement regarding such things, i.e. how these things are used by poets. We will ... not make the ... mistake of trying to test for judgement before the pupils have the requisite knowledge — thick or thin — to exercise their judgement upon (Winch and Gingell, 1996, p. 386).

Nevertheless teaching which largely directs itself towards the production by pupils of specific kinds of performance seems suspect for the following reasons. It is unlikely *adequately* to stimulate children to form appropriate connections between their concepts, to come to possess knowledge of which they have a measure of understanding, and for which they can provide some justification. Experience suggests that in the interests of short-term efficiency, especially given the pressure of league tables of test and examination results, teachers will acquire methods for bypassing the elusive idea of underlying knowledge and understanding, methods directly addressing the production of relevant performances. Some pupils, especially the more able, will themselves fill in the 'gaps'. The majority may be left with dislocated and isolated thin capacities which are likely to be quickly forgotten. Teachers whose objectives concerning knowledge and understanding have been distorted in the direction of the emulation of particular kinds of performance seem likely to lose sight of the richer, long-term aim. They will be much less inclined to come up with the wealth and range of activities, explanations and problems which stimulate understanding.

The second aspect of distortion I wish to discuss is the more important. It concerns how both teachers and pupils actually view the nature of the knowledge and understanding which is supposed to be learned. This in turn is linked to what Messick (1994), quoting Linn *et al.* (1991), and others refer to as the transparency or meaningfulness criterion in validity judgements.

> If the assessment itself is to be a worthwhile educational experience serving to motivate and direct learning, then the problems and tasks posed should be meaningful to the students . . . not only should students know what is being assessed, but the criteria and standards of what constitutes good performance should be clear to them in terms of both how the performance is to be scored and what steps might be taken or what directions moved in to improve performance (Messick, 1994, p. 16).

Those sympathetic to observations of this kind may still wonder whether they have anything to do with validity. Further remarks by Messick suggest that he sees the link in the following way. If pupils are clear about the standards and criteria for good performance, and if the same standards and criteria are applied in the teaching preceding the relevant assessment, then the aptitudes and traits which the assessment is designed to measure are more likely to develop. This appears to be an argument for a kind of self-fulfilling notion of validity. Design a test, make clear to the pupils the standards and criteria to be employed in the marking of the test, employ these standards in the teaching programme, and then the test is bound to measure what it is supposed to measure.

Of course, this still leaves open the question whether it is worth developing such aptitudes and traits. Moreover it can do nothing to spirit any of the range of putative psychological furniture into existence whose identity problems are intractable. We have already discussed such difficulties at length. Nevertheless, the criteria of transparency and meaningfulness themselves are relevant to the main argument, as we shall see. They suggest the contention that teachers and pupils ought to *share* a particular conception of the knowledge and skills which the pupils are supposed to be acquiring. This conception is not, of course, simply plucked from the air. Its character may be justified, as was suggested in Chapter 2 at least for the sake of the argument, by the needs of an industrial economy. That is to say, the knowledge should to a degree be understood, its possessors should be able to supply a measure of justification for it, and at least in some of the relevant senses they should be capable of using and applying it.

Yet teachers constrained by the pressures of league tables and the like, or by the desire to emulate portfolio exemplars in the interests of consistency and a shared understanding of the attainment descriptions, may actually be intending to 'teach' pupils to produce a limited range of closely defined performances. So it may be argued that one of the actions which they ought to take to maximise their chances of obtaining what they want from their pupils is to share with their pupils these short-term learning objectives.

However, if teachers do make a clean breast about what they are seeking to achieve they are distorting the proper purposes of education, even as judged by the instrumental criteria relating to an industrial economy. As a result some pupils may fail to acquire an adequate conception of knowledge. They will absorb the model of learning, and indeed of education more generally, being signalled to them by their teachers. They may, for example be perfectly content with a thin rule-bound conception of mathematics, to their great disadvantage. Moreover the industrial economy would seem unlikely to profit from pupils conceiving of their learning in this fashion.

Furthermore, there are ethical considerations here. If teachers actually intend pupils to produce relevant performances, it would be dishonest of them to convey the idea that their objectives are the development of richer knowledge and understanding. A kind of hypocrisy about the nature of what should be centre stage in the teaching and learning process would be detected by many pupils, and could prove gravely damaging to their own commitment to learning.

It may be thought that the envisaged cashing of general statements about knowledge and skills into exemplar tasks which we have been discussing so far is implausibly crude. No teacher would be satisfied, it might be objected, with any idea of an 'equivalence' between a general statement about attainment and just *one* illustrative task. The portfolio would rather contain a suitable *range* of tasks which would capture much more of the richness of the original statement. Thus the portfolio's contents would resemble the whole range of evidence which a teacher might accumulate about a pupil more informally, and on the basis of which she would judge that they possess particular kinds of knowledge, understanding and skill.

Although this move in some ways seems promising, problems remain. Would pupils have to match performances with all the 'different' exemplars? Or only some of them? Just how many different 'kinds' of tasks should be made paradigms? How do we decide on the extent of the diversity? Suppose pupils did poorly on some and rather better on the others purportedly relating to the same attainment statement. What do we do if equally experienced teachers or other experts disagree about which tasks 'fit' a particular statement of attainment? If this problem were circumvented by a nationally enforced reference set of exemplars, on what basis would these be chosen?

Perhaps it may be thought that these are simply practical difficulties. If so, I would also want to argue that the manoeuvre of increasing the size of the portfolios is ultimately a piece of superficial tinkering. The basic distortion of the meaning of the statements of attainment would remain. Knowledge and understanding simply cannot be equated with finite sets of performances. This remains the case even if it is insisted that the possession of a particular item of knowledge is to be identified with the fact that the pupil's performances match all of the several different types of exemplars stored in the portfolio against that knowledge item. For, given a dispositional/functional account of belief, virtually any behaviour can be thought of as manifesting the possession of a particular belief. This is because the appropriate interpretation will make assumptions about other 'connected' beliefs held by the agent and about relevant desires and intentions.

The denial that knowledge can be equated with finite sets of performances may seem familiar enough. Many have made seemingly related points in the long debate about the deficiencies of 'behaviourist' analyses. The point was touched on in Chapter 2. Thus Carr (1993) observes, 'far from . . . capacity requiring to be understood as the sum or product of dispositional competencies, the latter need understanding in terms of the knowledge base which characterises the former'. For Carr, 'dispositional competencies' relate to causal effectiveness, and to specifiable functions which may result from training or natural endowment, whereas 'capacity' relates to knowledge, and the 'voluntary and deliberate exercise of principled judgement in the light of rational knowledge and understanding'. I share Carr's view of behaviourist analyses, even though I am not quite certain about the use he makes of some of his terms.

Note also that if we discuss the possibility of requiring that portfolios contain a wider variety of types of exemplars, we are of course making free with the notion of 'kind' so heavily criticised earlier. Moreover we must remember that to ensure consistency or reliability the members of our larger collection of exemplars must be characterised in thin, physical and/or procedural terms.

Some may feel impatient with these proceedings as a whole. Even granting the above arguments, my expectations are simply too high, they would contend. We can obtain a measure of consistency, they might continue, while still succeeding in referring in some kind of way to knowledge and understanding.

My response is that the pressure for schools and other educational institutions to render themselves accountable through assessment is very strong. Much hangs on the results of assessment which affects the interests of pupils, students and teachers. It is a political decision to bring this pressure to bear, and the nature of learning, the language we use about it and the assessment techniques in principle available are insufficiently robust to sustain the required accountability. A National Curriculum framework, teacher assessment, and even some kinds of SATs might all have had the potential for contributing to the improvement of learning, were they not being wrenched into playing a part in a monitoring process which fails to grasp the nature of knowledge and learning itself.

RICH INTEGRATED COMPETENCIES AND THE ABILITIES OF STUDENT TEACHERS

Recent more sophisticated developments in thinking about competency might be held to undermine my objections to the possibility of a robust common criterion-referenced language about 'rich' knowledge and achievement. I now discuss a small selection of these in order to strengthen the main points I am seeking to make in this chapter. This discussion will also enable our treatment of assessment to be applied to a high-profile issue, namely competency-based assessment for student teachers.

Hager and Beckett (1995) defend what they describe as a holistic, integrated notion of competence, which may be inferred both on the basis of relevant performances, and on the basis of how the performer justifies and accounts for the performance and related actions. They oppose the kind of performance assessment that seeks to detect the presence of discrete physical skills one by one. Performance assessments of the type they favour are said to be increasingly popular. They cite the assessment of health-related professionals, of potential members of string quartets, and even of learner drivers by means of driving tests! Hager and Beckett are not directly and explicitly discussing the point at issue in this chapter, namely the difficulty of ensuring a shared meaning for statements about attainment. However, their thinking on the face of it is relevant to my concerns. For they claim that it is possible adequately to assess integrated, knowledge-rich competencies on the basis of modest selections of performance. If they are right, this could presumably support the consistency of criterion-referenced language.

They provide an intriguing illustration from the legal profession as it is practised in New South Wales (NSW). The Law Society of NSW rejected the idea of using traditional written examinations and referee reports to support the accreditation of specialist lawyers. In family law they felt that the conventional methods would not allow an adequate assessment of competencies which related to the quality of the interactions between the solicitor and the client, 'taking instructions and giving advice, assessing facts and legal options, canvassing the options with the client, and developing the initial plan'

(Hager and Beckett, p. 7). So candidates were asked to take part in simulated exercises involving the interviewing of a person playing the role of a client. The simulation is preferable to 'real' situations because of ethical considerations, but is made as 'realistic' as possible.

Hager and Beckett do not explicitly address the question of ensuring consistency of meaning in descriptions of the rich professional competencies which are involved. They do support the legitimacy of this kind of assessment; the candidates' performances in the simulations are presumably judged by practising professional lawyers. They claim that the integrated set of knowledge and understanding, practices and values which constitute professional practice may be seen as being acquired through 'cultural formation'. Inexperienced beginners learn through their participation in decision-making and judgements, in conjunction with experts and in the real contexts provided by the workplace. They will learn to recognise professional competencies in others. In the end, a particular competence 'is what a profession's peer group says it is' (*ibid.*, p. 12). Presumably this includes the claim that an individual has a particular professional competence if a group of relevant professionals says she does. So while consistency is not discussed, a reasonable degree of it must be assumed to be possible, or this type of competency discourse would and should fall into disrepute.

Hager's and Beckett's account is nicely consistent with the insights from the situated cognition tradition discussed earlier. The professional competencies cannot be conceptualised independently of workplace contexts. Hence assessment of such competencies is appropriately context-bound. They have not proceeded to draw negative conclusions about the ontological credentials of competencies of the kind I urged in relation to the insights of Goodman and the situated cognition tradition. However, they do seem to accept that there are problems about 'transfer':

> There seems to be empirical and conceptual support for generic competency within a professional field, with limited prospects for transferability. Part of the evidence for that is the agreements professional peers can and do reach about 'best practice'; there are individuals we have in mind when we make these generalisations. We can move beyond their role as models of best practice, but not so far as to uncouple the practice from its situation at that time and in that place (p. 15).

This narrative has an 'anti-realist' flavour. I think that we are being told that without the background of professional practices, the competencies simply would not 'exist'. In the legal case, for instance,

Hager and Beckett express themselves almost as though legal competencies only exist in so far as they are thought about by the lawyers. I am not clear whether they hold that competency discourse fails to 'cut nature at the joints', to echo Simon Blackburn (above p. 81). If they do, the question then arises as to whether there are in reality different 'joints' from those envisaged by the legal inventors of the competency descriptions, or whether the idea of 'joints' independent of knowers fails to make any kind of sense. The tone of their article to a degree suggests the latter.

The closest parallel between this law example and the education context would be the assessment of competencies in student teachers. For many years the 'professionals', that is teacher educators in higher education and teachers in school supporting students on placement, decided what a professional competence was. Medley (1984) speaks of the strong faith held by the profession in their capacity to judge the competence of new entrants on the basis of relatively brief observations. Drawing on the few studies available at that time, he concluded there was very little evidence that these judgements were predictors of teacher effectiveness (understood as the extent to which student teachers were responsible for appropriate improvements in pupil learning). He judged that it was as important for beginning teachers to *look* competent as to be competent, and that such evidence as existed did not point to any relationship between the two things.

None of this is very surprising. Suppose that there were specific teacher competencies which were causally implicated in the improvement of pupil learning. These would be manifested in a variety of ways across a range of classroom contexts. Imagine both that the possession of these competencies could be discovered, and that fine-grained short-term pupil learning improvements could be pinpointed and detected. (Both these suppositions are of course by implication denied in earlier argument.) Teacher trainers would be unlikely to be in a strong position to appraise the extent to which the student teacher's performance was actually implicated causally in this improvement. The quality and quantity of evidence available to the most conscientious of supervisors would be far too limited, apart from the difficulties in principle about discovering whether particular aspects of teacher behaviour have brought about pupil learning.

I would argue that we have not been sufficiently clear-sighted about the fact that the role of beginning teachers in bringing about pupil learning does not and cannot contribute in any significant way to judgements about the competencies of beginning teachers. The best defence teacher educators can offer of the claim that they can and do take account of pupil learning in their judgements about students might be the following: *experience* tells them what *kinds* of classroom behaviour on the part of teachers are 'likely' to stimulate learning. This move is unlikely to prove convincing to many, especially in view of the fact that many experienced and apparently 'adequate' teachers cannot be relied upon for 'methods that work' across the board.

There is a dangerous professional and intellectual vacuum here. It is being readily filled by those enthusiastic to use accountability for instrumental purposes. What constitutes a professional competence has become a contested issue. On the one hand are many practising teachers and teacher educators whose educational aims may be admirable but whose judgements about intending teachers are less than rigorous. On the other hand we have influential political groupings seeking to define the very nature of various professional competencies. They are determined to demand accountability in terms of them, relating these demands to learning outcomes and for relevant principles of procedure: 'the methods that work'.

It is only fair to note that before the dawn of competency-based student teacher assessment, many of those with the task of making judgements about student competencies, whether school-based or in Higher Education, would have defended a concern with far more than narrowly-defined learning outcomes. They would have claimed that their verdicts on student performance rested at least in part on conceptions of *education*, demanding special principles of procedure. They would have urged that their professional experience and skill did enable them to detect whether students were teaching according to these procedures, and that they could judge students accordingly on the basis of relatively brief observations.

In my view the damaging vacuum referred to above is inevitable. The debate may be characterised in the last analysis as a dispute over dispositions and traits (the alleged teaching competencies) many of which cannot properly be said to exist. Hence there is immense scope for irrationality, and for those in positions of power to have their way, regardless of whether all this activity has anything whatever to do with improving the qualities of beginning teachers, or more generally with 'raising standards'.

The reasons many of the traits cannot properly be said to exist are the same as those advanced against the kinds of traits supposedly underlying the transference of school knowledge to workplace competence. Bridges (1996) in his observations on competence-based teacher education does not refer to Hager and Beckett, but some of his thinking parallels theirs. He complains that the criticism of the competency approach is based on narrowly behaviourist versions of it. His versions of 'rich know-how' (not a phrase he uses), or approved competence 'constructs', incorporate generic higher-order competencies which involve 'deep structures of knowledge and understanding, a broad cognitive perspective, reflective and analytic capacity, sensitivity to relevant aspects of social or situational contexts, responsiveness'. While he acknowledges that there might be problems about how these competencies should be assessed, he judges that the approach in general 'rests upon more sophisticated and more acceptable epistemological assumptions' than a naive behaviourism.

It is difficult to disagree with Bridges in one sense, in that the kinds of achievements in which he is interested are the kinds that do strike us as significant and important for beginning teachers. If what he says could be taken in a loose sense as suggested summaries of what we hope and expect from teachers, all well and good. The problem is that he has apparently just 'invented' appropriate non-behaviourist competencies by collaging various desirable elements together and describing them as though they were traits which could be acquired and possessed over a period of time. He could not resist this accusation: such an invention is in fact an essential prerequisite for any kind of assessment of the said competencies. The thought has to be that the student teacher can acquire competencies which may be retained, and manifested in a wealth of different contexts. This whole manoeuvre of course simply sidesteps the arguments above about the problems of trait discourse and transfer, and hence must be rejected.

A similar criticism may be levelled at the kind of competencies which Hager and Beckett seek to defend, even if we value the kinds of assessment they favour. They are concerned, as has been said, to move right away from mere lists of 'thin' tasks, and to incorporate in their notion of competence a holistic perspective binding the situatedness of the performance with the knowledge and under-standing possessed by the pupil or student. They ask: 'what do the critics of integrated competence want? They imply that there is available some other way of deciding professional competence other than through a holistically-sensitive, collaborative and particularistic methodology, but we do not know what it is meant to be like' (p. 12).

There may be all kinds of arguments to support their approach to assessment. However, the authentic assessment of lawyers, for instance, has purposes differing fundamentally from the tough-minded accountability which is one of the themes of this book. Moreover trialling members of string quartets fortunately does not have to produce results which are 'comparable' between different quartets.

I referred to their paper not in order to disagree with all their contentions, but to explore the possibility of 'rich know-how' or 'integrated competence'. That possibility was discussed because it seemed to count against my main argument. I had contended that comparability of language and judgements about pupil achievement across teachers and schools, except in the case of reporting on the 'thinnest' type of knowledge, was not to be had in principle. Yet Hager and Beckett claim that 'rich know-how' can actually be detected by means of practicable performance assessment. If they are right about this, my pessimism about the prospects for comparability turns out to be ill-founded.

There are hints in their paper that Hager and Beckett think they have gone further in their development of the conception of rich integrated competencies than Bridges. Their intellectual ambitions seem to hinge upon the points about the cultural formation within professions of the judgements made about expertise and competence. They might feel that the discussion so far has not done justice to this aspect of their argument. Accordingly we will devote a little more space to the issue.

They tell us that cultural formation, undergone by the new professional through interactions with professional peers, contributes fundamentally to the judgements which are made about which knowledge is important, and indeed about the very nature of the reality as perceived by the professional group in question. The culturally defined beliefs, practices and judgements they describe seem to echo Searle's 'Background'.

However, Hager and Beckett make what I take to be a crucial concession when distinguishing between two kinds of profession. On the one hand we have professions such as law and accountancy which concern themselves with a professional culture addressing stable shared purposes. The related virtues 'fit an epistemological and ontological framework shaped by an acceptance of the *status quo*'. On the other hand we have, for instance, education and nursing, in which 'the territory of practice comes contested to the individual practitioner when the field is entered' (p. 5).

To the extent that the 'territory of practice comes contested' we arguably lose a vital kind of potential background support. Within education we do not have anything remotely approaching a homogeneity of practices, values and beliefs. If I have understood Hager and Beckett correctly such homogeneity helps lawyers, for instance, to make consistent assessments of intending entrants to their profession. Another way of capturing their view may be that the professionals define what counts as consistent (and valid) assessment.

Education, teaching and learning are complex value-suffused enterprises, within which professionals disagree about fundamental aims, and in consequence also dispute the appropriate roles for teachers and what counts as competent or effective teaching. This point also applies to any suggestion which might be made (in the style of Hager and Beckett) that within the cultural context of the school teachers could make consistent assessments of the extent to which pupils possess 'rich know-how' or 'integrated competencies'.

Incidentally, many politicians obviously dislike the value complexities and diversities prevailing within the education profession. In the UK, the National Curriculum together with its assessment apparatus and accountability requirements might be seen as a device for circumventing this pluralism, and insisting on the implementation of a specified set of values and practices. To achieve uniformity of practice, especially in respect of assessment, however, could only be achieved at the expense of rich knowledge. Yet, as we have seen, if there is such an achievement as rich knowledge, the industrial economy needs it.

To sum up, I have argued that specific kinds of 'rich know-how', attractive as they appear, are 'constructs' in an inappropriate sense. We are not able by ingenious use of language to summon up for them a clear identity over time and context. Further, the cultural embeddedness of judgements about the extent of rich know-how possessed either by student teachers or by pupils is not able to shore up criterion-referenced assessment language. Even if it could bring off this trick in a profession with an appropriate homogeneity of culture, practice and value, teaching lacks such a vital feature. Hence it is not possible for a common language to be used to characterise rich cognitive achievements by pupils in such a way that their attainments may be reported on in a wider arena and intelligible comparisons made.

Chapter 9
Is there a Future for Assessment and Accountability?

This book has concentrated on the limits of educational assessment, and in particular on the difficulties confronting current attempts to use educational assessment for accountability purposes. In this final chapter I want to look beyond these limits, and to comment briefly on what I would regard as wholly legitimate aims for assessment. In opposing a particular conception of accountability, I do not seek to oppose accountability *per se*, and I make some tentative remarks about alternative forms of accountability. If the school curriculum is not to be dominated by an inappropriate kind of accountability then there is a new opportunity for deeper reflections on what it might contain.

Much discussion in this book has turned on the assumption of an instrumental conception of education, at least as far as compulsory school provision is concerned. The natural bedfellow of such an instrumental conception of education is a tough regime in which accountability is rendered by the measurement of learning outcomes. However, the kinds of achievements in which industry seemed likely to interest itself, exemplified in Chapter 2's account of literacy and numeracy, have turned out to be singularly elusive. They resist accurate assessment. Rich knowledge and competencies would seem to be essential components, and yet such achievements turn out not to be the type of 'items' which can be acquired at school and then made use of in the variety of contexts afforded by adult life and employment. We have here, then, a fundamental objection to the kind of hard-nosed accountability for outcomes being insisted upon by a number of democratic states in the developed world. It follows that the vision of education as largely serving the needs of an industrial economy through the development of specific basic competencies is gravely flawed.

Pressure on schools which results from this catalogue of conceptual confusion arguably makes it *more* likely rather than less that pupils acquire qualities and dispositions which are neither useful nor desirable when they join the world of work. We have seen that the kinds of achievements which come closest to being susceptible of reasonably valid and reliable assessment, and nearest to being characterisable by a universal curriculum language, include the following: 'thin' or merely 'procedural' skills, and the possession of factual knowledge detached from the rest of the pupil's knowledge. Yet only a relatively small proportion of achievements of this kind are of any use to employers.

It is not, of course being claimed that teachers and others cannot gain *any* knowledge about their pupils' learning. Further, the common-sense intuition that schools can help their pupils to become numerate and literate remains unscathed, if it simply means that schools can help children to begin to understand numbers and their various applications, and to read and write. I have not sought to deny that the efforts of schools to make their pupils literate and numerate will make some broad differences to aspects of their performance at work. The aspects concerned could reasonably be thought of as related to literacy and numeracy. However, we need to be much more modest about how tightly our teaching efforts at school can possibly focus on competencies required in adult life. It is not possible for schools to teach literacy and numeracy in a fashion which is precisely directed to the 'needs' of industry. Instead, much more general education in these areas, whose precise outcomes cannot be quantified, remains on the agenda.

According to a Marxist analysis, concerns about the basics as expressed by government or industry, and the concomitant demand that education should be accountable through assessment, have little to do with faith in transfer. Although I do not intend to offer any support for such a position in this book, it is interesting to note how the sceptical view of fine-grained transfer fits this analysis quite neatly. John Beck comments:

> The educational qualifications which employers require as a condition of entry to jobs at various levels in the employment hierarchy, bear little relation — it is argued — to the skills which are actually needed in order to do those jobs efficiently. The real significance of educational qualifications (except at the highest levels) and the reason employers demand them, is first, that they function to legitimize the hierarchical ordering of social relations within the workplace, and second, that they are a guarantee that the applicant for the job has certain personal qualities such capitalism requires in its work force: obedience, diligence, etc. (1981, p. 103).

If there is any truth in these observations, it helps to explain the phenomenon discussed at the beginning of this book, namely the extraordinary persistence of assessment practices which are not only irrational, but apparently perceived as irrational by many in the developed world. Such a verdict is also depressing, in the sense that it reminds us of just how unlikely it is that policy decisions about assessment will be influenced by rational considerations.

The question whether there is a future for assessment and accountability within education can be considered afresh, once we are permitted to reflect once more on the ultimate aims of education, and the linked themes of the nature of the good society, the good life, and of what it is to be human. This book is not the place to engage in these debates. All I intend to do by way of concluding my discussion is offer a few pointers to the directions worth considering, if schooling in particular can rid itself of the shackles of an inappropriate accountability.

POSSIBILITIES FOR SCHOOLING NOT DOMINATED BY INSTRUMENTAL ACCOUNTABILITY

If school curricula were not dominated by those convinced of the possibility of fine-grained transfer, pupils might have more time to encounter the arts and humanities, so threatened in the 1990s educational provision of England and Wales. There might be compensations even in this for those so anxious about performance in the '3Rs'. It has been recently reported, for instance, that children exposed to certain kinds of music and art programmes between the ages of 5 and 7 can significantly improve their subsequent performance in maths (Gardiner, Fox, Knowles, and Jeffrey, 1996). Only a naive realist about transfer and possibilities of precision would be surprised by data of this kind.

If demands springing from an inappropriate version of accountability may be resisted, there is space once more for a consideration of what a modern democracy might want from its schools. People might once more be willing to consider the role of education in aiding citizens to keep under continual review the kind of society they wish to live in, the nature of personal happiness and the form of democracy important to them. Moreover there is also scope for more imaginative thinking about the kinds of personal qualities likely to contribute to an enterprise economy. It may be that there is a difference between what government thinks that industry requires from its employees, and what industry actually hopes for.

If the pressures on the education system from an inappropriately draconian accountability regime are removed, we can also look afresh at the issue of lifelong education. This would be timely, given the sentiments expressed in an important recent government report into Higher Education:

> 1.1 The purpose of education is life-enhancing: it contributes to the whole quality of life . . . In the next century, the economically successful nations will be those which become learning societies: where all are committed, through effective education and training, to lifelong learning.

1.10 The expansion of higher education in the last ten years has contributed greatly to the creation of a learning society, that is, a society in which people in all walks of life recognise the need to continue in education and training throughout their working lives and who see learning as enhancing the quality of life throughout all its stages. But, looking twenty years ahead, the UK must progress further and faster in the creation of such a society to sustain a competitive economy.

1.11 In a global economy, the manufacturers of goods and providers of services can locate or relocate their operations wherever in the world gives them greatest competitive advantage. Competitive pressures are reinforced by the swift pace of innovation and the immediate availability of information through communications technology. When capital, manufacturing processes and service bases can be transferred internationally, the only stable source of competitive advantage (other than natural resources) is a nation's people. Education and training must enable people in an advanced society to compete with the best in the world.

1.12 The pace of change in the work-place will require people to re-equip themselves, as new knowledge and new skills are needed for economies to compete, survive and prosper. A lifelong career in one organisation will become increasingly the exception. People will need the knowledge and skills to control and manage their own working lives.

1.13 This requires a learning society, which embraces both education and training, for people at all levels of achievement, before, during and, for continued personal fulfilment, after working life (DfEE, 1997).

This report is concerned with Higher Education, but its picture of the learning society has much wider implications. I have quoted it at some length since its opinions are entirely compatible with the *conclusions* of my book. The vision of a 'learning society' might well be thought to suggest that adults should be offered significant education or training by all employers, and that other educational opportunities should be made available on a regular basis during adulthood. The possibility that such lifelong education might be offered to all would permit a fundamental review of what should be offered in the *first* stages of education, namely during the period of compulsory schooling. Schools could be seen as appropriately fostering *general* cognitive development, together with certain vital personal qualities. Moreover if employers understood the limitations of transfer, they might have more sympathy with the wider preparation for adult life which schools might offer, and the work schools could do in helping pupils to acquire appropriate motivation, attitudes, stamina and the experience of working cooperatively with others. Employers might come to *expect* to offer very specific training and retraining to a much larger proportion of employees than they do at present. Such training would be designed to enable employees to perform according to certain standards in a given range of contexts. Employers would not complain that schools had failed to offer such training. Employers would understand that they require context-specific skills from their employees and that schools cannot normally supply these.

TEACHERS AS TECHNICIANS?

In making room for debate and ultimately for choices about the purposes of education, we allow teachers to be more than mere technicians implementing teacher- or pupil-proof teaching methods and content. However, in the UK there are already signs that teachers are beginning to lose their status as reflective professionals. They are instead acquiring roles as technicians who implement government policy not only on standards to be achieved but also on teaching methods to be employed. This issue was raised in Chapter 2. The 'Literacy Hour' is to be effectively compulsory in English primary schools. This refers to a highly prescriptive set of instructions for teaching young children to read and write. A 'Numeracy Hour' is in force from September 1999.

On the assumption that we wish to teach for understanding, and that we subscribe to a modest constructivist view of learning, it can be shown that the role of the teacher-technician is likely to fail pupils. Whether the teaching style is largely of an interactive whole-class character, or whether the teacher has more contact with groups and individuals, it must be flexible. The teacher needs to be able to react rapidly to unpredictable responses from pupils. If these reactions are heavily restricted by the 'manual', her capacity to provoke pupils into constructing new learning would seem to be severely impaired. It is surely essential that the teacher can draw on her own subtle and rich network of subject knowledge in these interactions. This knowledge should be supplemented by her professional experience, which will tell her something of the range of kinds of connections pupils tend to form, and of the nature of the diversity of pupil networks likely to be found in a typical group of a given age.

ACCOUNTABILITY AND 'STANDARDS'?

Nothing about the rejection of *certain* types of accountability for learning outcomes implies that schools should in no way be held to account. The populist cry 'we want value for money' may be accepted. The nub of the issue is, of course, what it is that is or should be valued. Those who are sceptical about 'accountability' are often accused of woolly-mindedness. My arguments neither legitimate woolly thinking by education professionals, nor the acceptance of poor 'standards'. Moreover they do not show that the pursuit of the 'basics' has no importance. However, the precise form that accountability in education should take, the content of the 'basics' and what counts as high standards can only be determined by an agreed set of fundamental purposes for education.

Certainly I have opposed the making of teachers and schools accountable for learning outcomes when the latter are identified with specified competencies and the possession of specific items of knowledge. It does not follow from this that we should not hold schools to account in a more general sense for the development of certain personal qualities in their pupils.

In deciding the form this accountability should take, we must have regard for the complexity and range of variables which impinge upon human learning, performances, motivation and attitude. It still should be possible for professionals to arrive at a consensus of a kind concerning educational aims and democratic ideals. Armed with this they could reach some agreement on at least the broad principles for teaching and learning styles and the selection of curriculum content most likely to enhance motivation, attitude and learning. If these 'principles' are explicit in school policies and inspection frameworks, I do not see why schools cannot be accountable for their implementation of such principles through rigorous inspections by appropriate professionals.

A FUTURE FOR ASSESSMENT?

Where does the argument leave educational assessment itself? I have criticised the use of assessment for accountability purposes. I have also questioned its role in supporting certain kinds of teaching styles involving substantial 'differentiation by task'. However, I still claim *that informal teacher assessment, in the form of interactions between teachers and individuals, and between teachers and groups or whole classes, in which the teacher notes how pupils are approaching a problem, or thinking about a concept is at the heart of teaching.* That is a sentiment supported by the original Task Group on Assessment and Testing (DES, 1988).

Why do I take this view, when I may seem to have removed some of the chief reasons for carrying out assessment? I cannot answer this question as a philosopher. In what follows, my tentative response involves empirical assumptions, and ultimately requires to be located within a coherent and defensible conception of education which I have not provided in this book.

If teachers relinquish the attempt to assess closely for the presence of specified cognitive achievement, they need not at the same time refrain from making assessments of their pupils' attitudes and motivation. They may be especially concerned with pupils' attitudes to the process of learning itself, though they will need to be very alert to the extent to which such attitudes are subject-specific. Indeed it could be very helpful to discover that pupils have positive views of some subjects, or even of specific aspects of some subjects, but negative views of other subjects or aspects of subjects. Nothing in the argument of this book implies that teachers cannot make at least broad judgements of this kind with some accuracy. Of course, teachers will have a lively sense of the ever-changing character of attitude and motivation. Teaching informed by knowledge of pupil attitudes will be 'better' than teaching not so informed. Teachers may be more accomplished in their presentation of material and activities to which pupils are likely to have positive attitudes. We do not need psychology or philosophy to tell us that such positive attitudes generally go with greater concentration, persistence, sensible behaviour, and with pupils better able to assimilate and to remember any relevant material.

Another important target for formative assessment is the elusive quality of imagination. It is a truism that teaching should, among other things, aim to stimulate the imaginations of pupils. At the same time it is difficult to define imagination, and even if a satisfactory account can be given of this quality, it may be subject-specific. Jane might display extraordinary imaginative qualities during her maths lessons, but have a very rigid and uninspired approach to art. A further complication is that 'imaginative' frequently carries a positive evaluation, though not universally. Michael Frayn once wrote of a child character that he was a very imaginative little boy, and that what he imagined was very boring (Frayn, 1967).

However, I want to argue that precision is not particularly important here. If a teacher in a fairly general way is assessing the qualities of imagination being displayed by his or her pupils, the information thus gained can only enhance the teacher's planning. Now it may well be true that what one teacher would think imaginative another would judge unfocused and erratic, and that there are no 'objective' ways of settling the issue between them. Nevertheless, arguably it is vital that teachers are alert to the extent to which their pupils are fluent in the production of ideas, to their pupils' 'capacities' to discern and to use connections between different ideas, and to their 'abilities' to go beyond traditional ways of approaching problems. These phenomena are broadly associated with 'imagination'. The terms 'capacities' and 'abilities' as used here need not be reified. They may be regarded as summarising a range of pupil responses.

I turn now to another use for educational assessment which escapes the strictures of this book. In their interactions with pupils, teachers will often glean information about the nature of pupil misunderstandings. While the range of confusions may strike those striving to impart maths and science to younger children to be almost limitless, nevertheless certain kinds of difficulties often arise. A grasp of these can help teachers when planning how to explain certain concepts to larger groups, or how to structure and sequence experiences and tasks which relate to such concepts. The insights into pupils' states of mind can serve to keep alive in the teacher a vivid awareness of his or her role in provoking pupils to construct new knowledge. As was pointed out above, the quality of the interactions, the kinds of challenges and questions that the teacher will put whether working with larger or smaller groups, can be suitably informed by such insights. Teachers are likely to make use of a more effective range of models and analogies, employ language which pupils can readily understand, and be better at engaging and maintaining interest if they have at least some idea of how their pupils think about the relevant concepts or subject matter.

How intensively teachers should assess pupils informally in order to retain this 'alertness' to the vagaries of individual knowledge construction would be a matter for empirical investigation. Probably the answer will vary from one teacher to another. Possibly some groups of pupils would be more demanding in this respect than others. Younger or less able pupils seem obvious candidates. It is likely that teachers would need quite regularly to refresh their acquaintance with the approach of individual pupils to important concepts.

There are still other forms of assessment which in a sense survive the argument presented in this book. In the first chapter we debated possible purposes for assessment, which included the wish to test the success levels of teachers and schools. This aim is corrupted if it is tied to the wrong kind of accountability. Yet I would wish to defend assessment of cognitive achievements in some guises.

For instance, I support a continuation of investigations into pupil attainments of the kind conducted in the UK fifteen to twenty years ago under the auspices of the Assessment of Performance Unit. Very large numbers of written tests, and also controlled practical tests, were carried out on children at certain ages, to explore their achievements in English, maths and other areas. Schools and children were not named, and the project purported to provide some insight into how much children of a given age knew and understood about key content.

In the light of my arguments, any results from this kind of survey need to be taken with a considerable pinch of salt. Yet the data still can be very useful to teachers despite this health warning. If teachers have in front of them the tasks set the children, the ways in which children were questioned about their knowledge, and the schedules for appraising any relevant performances, it can be interesting to know that only 45% of 11 year-olds succeeded on such and such a task. It may be a pointer, however fallible, to the success or otherwise of what the children are being offered by teachers and schools. What the data may lack in validity can to a degree be compensated for if the survey is a very large one. Tens of thousands of children failing to gain the correct answer to a question about fractions may be a symptom of a badly designed question. Or it may form evidence of a kind about how poorly children understand fractions. Obviously no insight is or could be gained about the idiosyncratic conceptual structures present in the minds of individual pupils making up a particular class. This would not prevent their teacher from reviewing her teaching of fractions in the light of the 'information' about the fractions performance of tens of thousands of children. An awareness that in all likelihood something was wrong with the typical scheme of work designed to teach fractions could be salutary. The teacher would not know the nature of the problem, but at least he or she would be prompted to scrutinise the conventionally recommended approaches to teaching the relevant concepts.

Data of the same kind repeatedly gathered over periods of several years can play a part in improving teaching and learning. Again, it is interesting if 11 year-olds a decade ago were better at a task apparently requiring punctuation knowledge than they were this year. All kinds of questions can and should be asked about the task. It may be very inadequate as a device for probing significant aspects of pupil knowledge about punctuation. School curricula may not have remained constant. Pupils may be reading less as a consequence of social and technological change. Nevertheless teachers may wish to discuss what if any efforts they should make to counteract this trend if they feel that the figures actually mirror their own experience of pupil competence. They can reflect in this way and adjust their teaching while being perfectly well aware of the inherent limitations of the assessment devices employed.

Bibliography

Adey, P., Shayer, M. and Yates, C. (1989), *Thinking Science: The Materials of the CASE Project* (Waltham-on-Thames, Nelson).

Armstrong, D. (1973), *Belief, Truth and Knowledge* (Cambridge, Cambridge University Press).

Bailey, C. (1980), The autonomous teacher, in: H. Sockett (ed.), *Accountability in the English Educational System* (London, Hodder & Stoughton).

Baker, G. and Hacker, P. (1985), *Wittgenstein: rules, grammar and necessity* (Oxford, Blackwell).

Baker, L. (1995), *Explaining Attitudes* (Cambridge, Cambridge University Press).

Bartram, D. (1990), Reliability and validity, in: J. R. Beech and L. Harding (eds), *Testing People* (Windsor, NFER/Nelson).

Beck, J. (1981), Education, industry and the needs of the economy, *Cambridge Journal of Education*, 11. 2, pp. 87–106.

Bennett, N., Desforges, C., Cockburn, A. and Wilkinson, B. (1984), *The Quality of Pupil Learning Experiences* (London, Erlbaum).

Blackburn, S. (1991), Losing your mind, in: J. Greenwood (ed.), *The Future of Folk Psychology* (Cambridge, Cambridge University Press).

Bloom, B. *et al.* (1956), *Taxonomy of Educational Objectives. I: Cognitive Domain* (London, Longmans).

Bridges, D. (1996), Competence-based education and training: progress or villainy? *Journal of Philosophy of Education*, 30. 3, pp. 361–376.

Burton, L. (1984), *Thinking Things Through: Problem Solving in Mathematics* (Oxford, Blackwell).

Butterfield, E., Slocum T. A. and Nelson, G. D. (1993), Cognitive and behavioural analyses of teaching and transfer: are they different? in: D. Detterman and R. Sternberg (eds), *Transfer on Trial: Intelligence, Cognition and Instruction* (Norwood, N.J., Ablex Publishing Corporation).

Cambridge Institute of Education (1985), *New Perspectives on the Mathematics Curriculum* (London, HMSO).

Carr, D. (1993), Question of competence, *British Journal of Educational Studies*, 41.3, pp. 253–271.

Carr, W. and Hartnett, A. (1996), *Education and the Struggle for Democracy* (Buckingham, Open University Press).

Cockcroft, W. *et al.* (1982), *Mathematics Counts* (The Cockcroft Report) (London, HMSO).

Cohen, L. and Manion, L. (1989), *Research Methods in Education* (London, Routledge).

Dancy, J. (1985), *Introduction to Contemporary Epistemology* (Oxford, Blackwell).

Davidson, D. (1970), Mental events, in: J. Swanson (ed.), *Experience and Theory* (Amherst, University of Massachusetts Press).

Davidson, D. (1973), Radical interpretation, *Dialectica*, 27, pp. 313–328.

Davidson, D. (1974), Belief and the basis of meaning, *Synthese*, 27, pp. 309–323.

Davis, A. (1986), Learning and belief, *Journal of Philosophy of Education*, 20. 1. pp. 7–20.

Davis, A. (1988), Ability and learning, *Journal of Philosophy of Education*, 22. 1, pp. 45–55.

Davis, A. (1990), Logical defects of the TGAT report, *British Journal of Educational Studies*, 38. 3, pp. 237–250.

Davis, A. (1993), Matching and assessment, *Journal of Curriculum Studies*, 25. 3, pp. 267–279.

Davis, A. (1995), Criterion-referenced assessment and the development of knowledge and understanding, *Journal of Philosophy of Education*, 29. 1, pp. 3–23.

Davis, A. (1996a), Who's afraid of assessment? Remarks on Winch and Gingell's reply, *Journal of Philosophy of Education* 30. 3, pp. 389–400.

Davis, A., (1996b), To add value, first confuse the parents, *Times Educational Supplement*, September 27th, p. 24.

Davis, A. (1997), Understanding mathematics, *Journal of Philosophy of Education*, 31. 2, pp. 355–364.

Dearden, R. (1968), *The Philosophy of Primary Education* (London, Routledge & Kegan Paul).

Denvir, B. and Brown, M. (1986), Understanding of number concepts in low attaining 7–9 year olds, *Educational Studies in Mathematics*, 17, pp. 15–36.

DES (1985), *Better Schools* (London, HMSO).

DES (1988), *National Curriculum Task Group on Assessment and Testing. A Report* (London, HMSO).

Detterman, D. K. (1993), The case for the prosecution: transfer as an epiphenomenon, in: D. K. Detterman and R. J. Sternberg (eds), *Transfer on Trial: Intelligence, Cognition and Instruction* (Norwood, N.J., Ablex Publishing Corporation).

DFE (1995a), *English in the National Curriculum* (London, HMSO).

DFE (1995b), *Mathematics in the National Curriculum* (London, HMSO).

DfEE (1997), *Higher Education in the Learning Society* (available on the Internet: http://www.ncl.ac.uk/ncihe/natrep.htm).

Dummett, M. (1973), *Frege: Philosophy of Language* (New York, Harper & Row).

Ernest, P. (1991), *The Philosophy of Mathematics Education* (London, Falmer).

Flew, A. (1987), *Power to the Parents* (London, Sherwood Press).

Flew, A. (1995), *Class Action* (London, The Adam Smith Institute).

Fodor, J.A. (1991), Fodor's guide to mental representation, in: J. D. Greenwood (ed.), *The Future of Folk Psychology* (Cambridge, Cambridge University Press).

Fodor, J. and Lepore, E. (1992), *Holism: A Shopper's Guide* (Oxford, Blackwell).

Frayn, M. (1967), *Towards the End of the Morning* (London, Penguin).

Gardiner, M., Fox, A., Knowles, F. and Jeffrey, D. (1996), *Nature*, 381 No. 6580, p. 284.

Gettier, E. (1963), Is justified true belief knowledge? *Analysis*, 23, pp. 121–123.

Grice, P. and Strawson, P. (1956), In defence of a dogma, *Philosophical Review*, 65.

Goodman, N. (1970), Seven strictures on similarity, in: L. Foster and J. Swanson (eds), *Experience and Theory* (London, Duckworth).

Greeno, J., Moore, J., and Smith, D. (1993), Transfer of situated learning, in: D. Detterman and R. Sternberg (eds), *Transfer on Trial: Intelligence, Cognition and Instruction* (Norwood, N.J., Ablex Publishing Corporation).

Haack, S. (1978), *Philosophy of Logics* (Cambridge, Cambridge University Press).

Hager, P. and Beckett, D. (1995), Philosophical underpinnings of the integrated conception of competence, *Educational Philosophy and Theory*, 27. 1, pp. 1–24.

Hamlyn, D. (1967), The logical and psychological aspects of learning, in: Peters, R. (ed.), *The Concept of Education* (London, Routledge & Kegan Paul).

Hamlyn, D. (1978), *Experience and the Growth of Understanding* (London, Routledge & Kegan Paul).

Harré, R. (1978), Powers, in: R. Tuomela (ed.), *Dispositions* (Dordrecht, D. Reidel).

Harré, R. (1986), *Varieties of Realism* (Oxford, Blackwell).

Hirst, P. (1967), The logical and psychological aspects of teaching a subject, in: R. Peters (ed.), *The Concept of Education* (London, Routledge & Kegan Paul).

Jackson, F. (1977), *Perception* (Cambridge, Cambridge University Press).

James, M. and Conner, C. (1993), Are reliability and validity achievable in National Curriculum assessment? Some observations on moderation at Key Stage 1 in 1992, *The Curriculum Journal*, 4. 1, pp. 5–19.

Jennings, S. and Dunne, R. (1997), *T3 Mathematics. Towards Quality in Mathematics Teaching*. (Exeter University: available on the Internet: http://www.ex.ac.uk/telematics/maths/mathhpag.htm).

Jonathan, R. (1997), *Illusory Freedoms: Liberalism, Education and the Market* (Oxford, Blackwell).

Kripke, S. (1982), *Wittgenstein on Rules and Private Language* (Oxford, Basil Blackwell).

Lave, J. and Wenger, E. (1991), *Situated Learning: Legitimate Peripheral Participation* (New York, Cambridge University Press).

Lewis, D. (1974), Radical interpretation, *Synthese*, 27, pp. 331–344.

Linn, R., Baker, E. and Dunbar, S. (1991), Performance-based assessment: expectations and validation criteria, *Educational Researcher*, 20. 8, pp. 5–21.

Medley, D. (1984), Teacher competency testing and the teacher educator, in: L. G. Katz and J. D. Raths (eds), *Advances in Teacher Education* (Norwood, N. J., Ablex Publishing Corporation).

Messick, S. (1994), The interplay of evidence and consequences in the validation of performance assessments, *Educational Researcher*, 23. 2, pp. 13–23.

Moss, P. (1992), Shifting conceptions of validity in educational measurement: implications for performance assessment, *Review of Educational Research*, 62. 3, pp. 229–258.

Oakeshott, M. (1972), Education: the engagement and its frustration, in: R. F. Dearden, P. H. Hirst and R. S. Peters (eds), *Education and the Development of Reason* (London, Routledge & Kegan Paul).

Prais, S. J. (1995), Improving school mathematics in practice, in: *Proceedings of a Seminar on Mathematics Education* (London, Gatsby Charitable Foundation).

Prior, E. (1985), Dispositions (Aberdeen, Aberdeen University Press).

Putnam, H. (1970), Is semantics possible? in: H. Kiefer and M. Munitz (eds), *Language, Belief and Metaphysics* (New York, State University of New York Press).

Quine, W. (1953), *From a Logical Point of View* (Cambridge, Mass., Harvard University Press).

Quine, W. (1960), *Word and Object* (Cambridge, Mass., MIT Press).

Reznek, L. (1991), *The Philosophical Defence of Psychiatry* (London, Routledge).

Rust, J., and Golombok, S. (1989), *Modern Psychometrics* (London, Routledge).

Ruthven, K. (1988), Ability stereotyping in mathematics, *Educational Studies in Mathematics*, 18.

Ryle, G. (1949), *The Concept of Mind* (London, Hutchinson).

SCAA (1996), *Key Stage 2 Assessment Arrangements* (Hayes, SCAA Publications).

Searle, J. (1980), *Expression and Meaning* (Cambridge, Cambridge University Press).

Searle, J. (1992), *The Rediscovery of the Mind* (Cambridge, Mass., MIT Press).

Singley, M. and Anderson, J. (1989), *The Transfer of Cognitive Skill* (Cambridge, Mass., Harvard University Press).

Skemp, R. (1989), *Mathematics in the Primary School* (London, Routledge).

Sklar, L. (1980), Semantic analogy, *Philosophical Studies*, 38, pp. 217–234.

Sockett, H. (1980), Accountability: the contemporary issues, in: *Accountability in the English Educational System* (London, Hodder & Stoughton).

Stenhouse, L. (1975), *An Introduction to Curriculum Research and Development* (London, Heinemann).

Thorndike, E. (1906), *Principles of Teaching: Based on Psychology* (New York, Seiler).

Thorndike, E. (1914), *The Psychology of Learning* (New York, Teachers College Press).

Times Educational Supplement (1997b), Report on poor standards of Japanese literacy, January 10th, p. 19.

Times Educational Supplement (1997b), My best teacher, July 18th, p. 18.

Williams, K. (1992), *Assessment: A Discussion Paper* (Dublin, Association of Secondary Teachers).

Winch, C. and Gingell, J. (1996), Educational assessment: reply to Andrew Davis, *Journal of Philosophy of Education*, 30. 3, pp. 377–388.

Wittgenstein, L. (1958), *Philosophical Investigations* (Oxford, Blackwell).

Index